UBUNTU

On Whose Shoulders We Stand

TERERAI TRENT

KMD
BOOKS

A catalogue record for this
work is available from the
National Library of Australia

National Library of Australia Catalogue-in-Publication data:
Ubuntu/Tererai Trent

ISBN:
978-0-6457858-4-5
(Paperback)

ISBN:
978-0-6458670-3-9
(Hardback)

CONTENTS

FOREWORD

SARAH FERGUSON, DUCHESS OF YORK

D r Tererai Trent's collection of stories speaks to what I have always believed in life—our humanity is connected when kindness shines through and there is a deep bond that's formed between people and among nations when they feel seen and valued. I have followed Dr Trent's work ever since I first read some of her writing. I love how she creates a beautiful world through education.

I'm delighted to write the foreword for this book, *Ubuntu: On Whose Shoulders We Stand*, an anthology written by Tererai Trent and an amazing group of phenomenal women.

Dr Trent's anthology comprises of remarkable lived experiences that not only warm our hearts, but also inspire us to be the shoulders that others can stand upon. I'm truly inspired to see a cadre of women honoring and celebrating the heroines and sheroes who paved the path to their dreams, especially during the most challenging times of their journeys.

Without a shadow of doubt, Tererai believes that the chances of achieving our dreams in life are greater when our passion for them collides with others who believe and support us.

While each story celebrates the heroes and sheroes who paved the way for these women, these lived experiences offer life lessons for global healing while nurturing the essence of our humanity that exists inside us all.

Tererai, my friend, please accept my gratitude for sharing ubuntu with the world. Thank you for allowing us to stand on each other's shoulders.

To the authors in this book, thank you for your brave voices and for tapping into what makes us human beings—ubuntu. Indeed, as your stories crystalize the essence of our humanity, this is what ultimately heals the world.

Sarah Ferguson, Duchess of York

INTRODUCTION

TERERAI TRENT

'I almost gave up my dreams as I pursued them. The challenges were insurmountable; I faced a dark, treacherous and invisible road in my dream life until others helped me to navigate the most difficult terrain of my journey.'
—*Tererai Trent*

*U*buntu: On Whose Shoulders We Stand is a collection of stories written by phenomenal women honoring the heroes and sheroes who have paved the path for them to accomplish their dreams, especially during the most challenging times of their journeys.

This collection by women celebrates unsung individuals, and not only inspires this generation and future generations, but also teaches us to live a life of legacy based on gratitude.

The English scientist Sir Isaac Newton once wrote, "If I have seen further, it is by standing on the shoulders of giants." Indeed, supported by the African philosophy of ubuntu, we are who we are because of others who believe in us. That is the essence of humanity, and this is what gives meaning to life because our humanity is deeply connected to one another.

Unfortunately, we live in a world that celebrates individual success while diminishing the role others play in achieving our dreams. We often hear, "I lifted myself up by my own bootstraps." While there are many heroes and heroines who paved the way to achieve my dreams, a life-defining moment with a stranger, Jo Luck, pretty much changed the trajectory of my life. Sitting on the bare ground, Jo Luck asked me a question during the most difficult time of my life: "What are your dreams?" This question took me on an unforgettable journey and changed not only my life but also generations.

By the age of eighteen, with no formal education, I was the mother of four children, married to an abusive man. Equally challenging, I had grown up under a colonial system of governance that had oppressed my people for many decades. As a young mother with little education, I lived in poverty.

These influences in my early life silenced me. Like many other women, I was racing to self-destruction, running a relay that I had never signed up for. With my wounds intact and yet exposed for the world, I ran bearing the batons of illiteracy, of early marriage and of fear—the fear of leaving an abusive relationship.

However, given the encounter with Jo Luck, and the encouragement from my mother and grandmother, I wrote down my five dreams on an old scrap of paper: 1. To go to America, 2. To earn a bachelor's degree, 3. To earn a master's degree, 4. To earn a doctorate and 5. To improve the lives of women and girls in my community so they wouldn't have to experience what I had gone through in my life. I sealed the list of dreams in an old tin can and buried it under a rock in the place where I used to herd cattle. Despite numerous setbacks, I never lost sight of my dreams, and achieved not only my dreams. At the end of her TV show, Oprah Winfrey named me her "all-time favorite guest". Without others on whose shoulders I stand, I wouldn't have achieved this level of success. Today, with nine other women, including Jane Goodall, I am immortalized in a life-size bronze figure in the United States. My statue was unveiled on Women's Equality Day on 26 August 2019.

It's important to keep in mind that our ability to effectively navigate the invisible stretch of road is improved if we look to those who have gone before us, pioneering leaders and everyday heroines, for inspiration and guidance. May we remember these people and celebrate their unwavering support in allowing us to stand on their shoulders. May we celebrate them as midwives for the awakening of the next generation and the world's healing. Indeed, this collection creates a platform to celebrate those who have helped us achieve our dreams.

Distinguished as Oprah's "all-time favorite guest", Dr Trent is a scholar, humanitarian, motivational speaker, educator, mentor and founder of Tererai Trent International. She is the author of the award-winning *The Awakened Woman – Remembering & Reigniting Our Sacred Dreams*. Tererai also serves as the president of The Awakened Woman, LLC, a company dedicated to empowering women with tools to thrive as they achieve their dreams.

A LASTING IMPRESSION

SCHARRELL JACKSON

I t is a frequent inquiry, the story of a black woman rising through the ranks of a predominantly male industry and transitioning into entrepreneurship. Reflecting on my trajectory, I am bathed in gratitude for the inspirational leaders who have been my pillars of strength and support. Among these luminous figures, one that has had a profound impact on my identity is my grandmother, Lillie.

The very utterance of her name evokes immense affection and respect within me. Not to undervalue my maternal grandmother's contribution, a matriarch to a sprawling clan of eleven children and over a hundred grandchildren and great-grandchildren, including me. Her capacity to provide individual attention was understandably stretched, considering her youngest child was merely four months older than me.

But it was Lillie, my paternal grandmother, who became the touchstone of my life. She sowed the seeds of confidence and self-belief within me during my early years, a time when I was wrangling with my own insecurities. In ways subtle and overt, she influenced my development, and it was her steadfast faith in me that eventually blossomed into the self-assured woman I became.

Reflecting further on my grandmother Lillie's influence, I recall her as my bedrock of strength and inspiration. From my earliest memories, she instilled a powerful conviction within me that I could manifest any dream, any ambition, no matter how grand. Her words of affirmation acted as my shield in moments of insecurity and self-doubt, empowering me to pursue anything, regardless of the obstacles ahead.

As a child, my curiosity was often perceived as talkativeness; my inquisitiveness was misconstrued as an annoyance. Yet, Grandma Lillie, amidst the clamor of misunderstandings, recognized my potential. She viewed my endless questions as a marker of intelligence and foresaw in me the qualities of a leader. At that tender age of two or three, her words were beyond my comprehension. However, in retrospect, I understand that she was the first to acknowledge the potency of my voice.

Even in times when my voice seemed muffled and when I lacked the confidence to articulate my thoughts, it was her belief in me that echoed into my mind. I remember being a tiny tot in a store, perplexed by the peculiarity of an orange being called "orange" while an apple wasn't known as "red". It was then that she assured me my questions and my curiosity were valid, marking the early signs of the leader I would become.

Lillie treated my childlike curiosity with dignity, encouraging my desire to explore the world around me. Questions that would flummox an average adult—"How does electricity illuminate a bulb?" or "Why does the leak stem from there when the water is here?"—were met with nurturing patience. At no point did she make me feel inadequate or unusual, sensations that, regrettably, shadowed much of my childhood. Instead, she validated my curiosities, recognizing them as the driving forces behind a lifelong passion for learning and sharing knowledge.

She was more than a grandmother; she was my courage incarnate, the dream-weaver who breathed life into my aspirations. It wasn't until my emotional maturity that I grasped the profound impact of her presence. Her tales of overcoming adversities, her relentless determination and her resilience propelled me forward when my journey was punctuated by hardships. I was dealt the most significant blow when I lost Lillie the day

I welcomed my first child into the world.

She was hit by a car and killed as a result while walking my cousin to school. At that very moment, unbeknownst to me, I was in the throes of labor. Yet, consumed by grief for the matriarch I was about to lose, I was oblivious to the physical pain. That night, my water broke, and by the following morning, I was cradling my newborn son, Donavon. I believe that my grandmother transferred her soul to him. Thus, I carry a piece of Lillie within me, channeling her indomitable spirit through Donavon.

Lillie remains a beacon of motivation and inspiration. She lives on as a testament to her impact and her power to shape a young mind and heart. We all have the potential to be a "Lillie" to someone, nurturing their curiosity, bolstering their confidence and inspiring them to dream.

My mother, Deborah, was the eldest girl among eleven children, finding herself in a matronly role from an early age. A surreal reality where her youngest sister was the same age as her own child—me. Amid the clamor of an expansive family, my mother shared her childhood with me. One can only imagine the trials of a nineteen-year-old girl wrestling with the burden of premature motherhood and yearning for liberation from incessant responsibilities.

As fate would have it, she conceived me at the young age of nineteen. I still recall the chilling echo of the words, "I never wanted kids anyway," uttered when I was merely four years old. Those words felt like a sledgehammer to my spirit, instilling in me an overwhelming need to overachieve, to please, to earn the love I believed was withheld.

This drove me into a cycle of overdoing everything—over-questioning, over-contributing and always striving to fit in and be wanted. It was this relentless pursuit of validation that unwittingly shaped me into the successful person I am today.

Parallel to my mother's narrative, my grandmother was a continuous source of affirmation. Until the age of sixteen, every weekend was spent in her comforting presence, each moment filled with learning and exploration. There, I was not the "too loud" or "overbearing" child as painted by my mother; I was simply Scharrell.

In my quest to be accepted by my mother, I strove to become the daughter I thought she desired. This included becoming a protective older sister to my brother, who was only eleven months younger. The urge to excel resonated throughout my academic life as I consistently outperformed my peers.

Despite the hardships of my early years, I came to realize that I was standing on my mother's shoulders. Her struggles and sacrifices became stepping stones that unknowingly shaped my resilience and determination.

My mother's life became a testament to perseverance, a vivid portrait of an arduous journey from poverty to success. This narrative was less about her feelings towards me but rather reflected the burdens she shouldered from her own past. Unprepared and unexpectedly propelled into motherhood, she faced a deluge of adversities, yet she held firm. Even though she uttered words of regret, her actions bore witness to a fierce maternal instinct.

The echo of her confession served as a catapult, launching me into a relentless pursuit of achievement. While initially driven by a need to prove my worth, this journey instilled a sense of determination and unwavering consistency toward my goals. As I matured and built a deeper relationship with my mother, I began to comprehend the backdrop against which those words were spoken—it was a reflection of her hardships rather than her sentiment towards me.

Her resilience as a single mother, her unwavering faith in God and her relentless struggle against adversity became my blueprint for strength. Today, she is my loudest cheerleader, my closest confidante and my strongest advocate. Even though her words once crushed my self-esteem, they made me resilient. They transformed me into a person who perseveres, constantly striving for acceptance. Hence, I can say with certainty that I stand tall on my mother's mighty shoulders, thriving on her lessons of resilience.

My mother relentlessly pursued her education, becoming one of the first in her family to graduate from college. Her journey did not stop there, as she climbed the ladder of success, later marrying my stepfather. But perhaps the most significant lesson from my mother was that of giving. She was always offering support to her family. At times, I felt sidelined, secondary to her siblings and parents. However, it dawned upon me that she was teaching me the importance of family, of putting others before oneself.

I recall when our three-bedroom apartment was bustling with life, housing me, my mother, her siblings and her mother all under the same roof. Despite the cramped quarters, it was home. It was a testament to my mother's sacrifices and her belief in the significance of family. Regardless of our circumstances, we were never made aware of our poverty.

My mother, throughout her life, has personified the virtue of selfless giving. Indeed, her entire existence has been a testament to the power of love and sacrifice. It was only recently that I had to summon the strength to ask her to pause. As the matriarch of our family, she had shouldered the weight of our lives for so long that the sight of her aging sparked an urgent need within my brother and me to relieve her of her burdens.

As a single mother of three kings for twenty years, I recognize the enormity of my mother's struggle. My mother's influence has shaped my spirit; her sacrifices have become the blueprints for my resilience, and her love is the cornerstone of my strength.

Through her life, I found a lesson of fortitude and generosity. We are reminded that it's not about the hardships we face but how we rise above them that defines us. It shows us that our interactions, no matter how challenging they may seem, can have a positive and significant impact on our lives. In understanding the nuances of my mother's story, we learn to acknowledge the profound influence the people closest to us have on our journey.

Insecurity, a shadowy companion, often leads us down paths of ill judgment, and like a puppeteer, you can make moves without thought. I found myself making poor decisions when it came to relationships early in life, focusing on pleasing versus my self-worth. When insecurity takes the helm, it can steer even the most brilliant minds into the tempest of poor decisions. As an academic standout, leaping over grades and graduating early, I still found myself navigating rough waters in my relationships. This was due, in large part, to my inability to recognize the true form of love. At an incredibly tender age, I became ensnared in a web of relational dysfunction.

Beneath the veneer of accomplishment—working since age thirteen and being a full-charge bookkeeper by college—I was a duality personified. Outwardly, I was the epitome of strength, but inside, I was wrestling with silent anguish. As a teenager and young adult, I was lost in the labyrinth of relationships, making wrong turns, choosing the wrong companions and consequently suffering severe traumas.

However, life has a beautiful way of introducing saviors at the darkest hours. For me, it was Patricia, affectionately known as "Sister Weaver". It was at a Women Reaching Women Bible study that I first broke my silence, voicing the torment that had held me captive for so long. In that sacred space, I shared the traumatic experiences that had hitherto cast a pall over my life.

Sister Weaver guided me through the healing process, not only in confronting the aftermath of my past traumas but also in healing the wound that seared into my heart. The journey with Sister Weaver was transformative, and it helped me realign my perception. I was not the sum of my past experiences; rather, they were stepping stones toward the person I was destined to be. My traumas morphed from painful memories into catalysts for personal growth, propelling me toward the best version of myself.

With Sister Weaver in my life, walking me through each step of healing, I found myself fostering a profound relationship with Jesus Christ. Consequently, I grew stronger, more authentic and more transparent. The heavy shroud of shame that had weighed me down finally lifted, freeing me to fully embrace my life with God.

I learned the power of choice—that my life, my future and my destiny were all in God's hands. I understood I had every right to experience, feel and live my life the way I chose. This realisation lead me to harness my vulnerability and transform my wounds into tools of healing for others.

In the throes of insecurity, even the brightest minds can be led astray. I am infinitely grateful to Sister Weaver. She was not just a guide but also a beacon of hope, leading me from the edge of despair toward healing. Not only did it involve addressing specific traumatic incidents but also tending to deep-seated emotional wounds from childhood.

She gave me the courage to rise above my circumstances, encouraging me to lean on her strength when I lacked my own, emphasizing the necessity of support networks in our healing process, which serves as a testament to the power of companionship. Our wounds can transform into tools of healing for others. Healing is a journey, not a destination, and it is far-reaching.

The power of love's true form is invaluable and key to forging healthy relationships. This is a sobering reminder that self-worth and confidence play an essential role in decision-making. Her unwavering support propelled me through a journey that not only yielded strength and power but also freed me from the chains of guilt and shame, instilling hope.

We often believe as parents that our children lean on us, but I found myself leaning on my three kings—my sons. They allowed me space to be who I needed to be, making sacrifices along the way and embodying patience as their mother navigated life's tumultuous seas. The kids I invited into our home, those souls I dared to claim as my own, became surrogate siblings to my sons. I recognize now how much my kings sacrificed, not for their own sake, but for others. They let me be me, and for that, I am forever grateful. My greatest accomplishment is not my professional success but my three wonderful sons, my kings, upon whose shoulders I proudly stand.

THE STORY OF RUSS

Navigating the seas of my early career, I found myself entrenched in male-dominated industries. From construction, manufacturing and distribution to professional services, each arena proved a challenge. Still, my determination sparked a steady climb through the ranks, leading me to achieve roles of significance—partner, chief financial officer and chief operations officer, ranking number two in the organisation. My success was groundbreaking, shattering the ceiling as an African-American woman in a world where such presence was less than 1% in the industries I served. Yet, this triumph wasn't without its shadows.

Despite the accolades, the higher I climbed, the more apparent the isolation became. I wasn't invited to the table for who I was but for what I brought to it. I yearned for a genuine sense of belonging and acceptance unattached to my credentials. During this turbulent period, Russ arrived in my life, a lighthouse amidst my storm.

Russ offered "clarity conversations", guiding me through my uncertainties and fears. With his wisdom, he painted a vivid tapestry of my future, easing my anxieties and promising a better tomorrow. His words resonated deep within me, helping me understand my journey and believe in the potential for a brighter future.

He looked at me, a caterpillar admired but confined, and saw the butterfly I could become. His unwavering belief inspired me, propelling me to embrace my potential and transform into the butterfly he saw within me. Russ provided a safe haven, allowing me to express my vulnerabilities and lean into my emotions. He transcended the role of a mentor or coach, becoming my confidante and guide.

From Russ, I learned about empathy, understanding and the

importance of meeting people where they are. His influence fostered a seismic shift in my leadership approach. From being a high-performing, demanding boss, I transformed into a leader who merged business acumen with grace and humility. He breathed confidence into me, fostering my belief in my potential and clearing my path toward entrepreneurship.

As I grappled with the challenges of being a single parent, juggling my roles as a business leader and a mother, Russ stood by me. His guidance lightened the sacrifices I made, supporting me as I grew as a businesswoman and a mother.

Now, as I stand tall amidst my life's trials, I do so on Russ' shoulders. His influence on my life is immeasurable, his guidance a beacon of hope and strength. Our journey together is a testament to the transformative power of a single individual and a reminder that we all have the potential to positively impact someone's life.

In 2019, my life took an unexpected turn. I suffered a stroke, a stark reminder of my mortality and the toll my relentless pursuit had taken on my health. The incident served as a wake-up call, compelling me to prioritize my well-being. Now, I refuse to leave God's gifts for me unwrapped on the shelf. My life story, my trials and tribulations, I offer them to encourage and motivate other women. It is my life's mission to show them that no matter what they've been through, they can rise above it all. They can experience life at its highest level if they just make the choice. As I always say, life is a choice, and your destiny is up to you, no matter what you've been through.

My journey has been a tapestry woven with strands of struggle, success, sacrifice and triumph. My story is not solely mine, but a collective saga of many remarkable souls whose shoulders I have had the privilege to stand upon. From the unwavering love of my grandmother, Lillie, to the fierce resilience of my mother, Deborah, and the guiding wisdom of Sister Weaver, the foundation of my journey has been fortified by these formidable women.

Russ, my professional mentor, showed me the intricacies of business, revealing the delicate dance between strength and vulnerability in leadership. It was upon his shoulders I learned the power of compassion in the corporate world, a lesson that forever transformed my professional journey.

I discovered that life's trials and tribulations are not insurmountable obstacles but catalysts for transformation. I learned to accept the support of others, to lean on them and to stand on their shoulders. And in the arms of my tribe—women like Trina, Maria, Deirdre and Dara—I found the courage to become an entrepreneur. Their support, both in prayer and practice, saw me through the highs and lows of entrepreneurship, reminding me of the power of the community of sisterhood.

Yet, in my personal life, the greatest testament to my being remains my three kings—my sons. They graciously bore the weight of their mother's dreams and struggles, allowing me to transform into the woman I am today. Their sacrifices, their unconditional love, has been my North Star through the darkest nights.

My journey is a testament to the power of choice, the potency of destiny and the transformative magic of perseverance. To every woman reading my story, know this: you are capable of extraordinary things. Your destiny is your own, a beacon of light only you can ignite. It doesn't matter what you've been through or where you come from; your future is a radiant dawn waiting to break. Choose to rise. Choose to stand tall. Choose your destiny, for life is indeed a choice.

Life has a way of introducing us to guiding lights during our darkest hours. Through the retelling of my journey, I hope to inspire you. Authenticity, transparency and strength are borne out of embracing one's own truth. There's immense liberation and growth in lifting the weight of shame and embracing oneself fully. I hope to invoke a sense of limitless potential, a newfound resilience and an unwavering belief in your power to shape your destiny. For in the grand tapestry of life, we all stand on the shoulders of giants. Let their strength bolster you, their wisdom guide you and their love uplift you. Stand tall, for your story is just beginning. May this chapter of my life serve as a testament to the transformative power of choice, resilience and unwavering faith, leaving you forever changed and infinitely empowered.

Scharrell Jackson

S charrell Jackson is an accomplished international keynote speaker and leadership coach. Leveraging over twenty-five years of executive experience, she specialises in elevating leaders to their highest level of success. She is best known for her unconventional and custom approach that ignites the fire in leaders, converting ambiguity into clarity, insecurity into confidence and fear into courage, yielding high-performance leaders through incredible breakthroughs.

Scharrell has served as a chief operations officer, chief financial officer and chief administrative officer across a wide range of industries, including fintech, manufacturing and distribution, non-profits, professional services, real estate, construction, technology and wealth management. She drives strategy, profit improvement, mergers and acquisitions, operational efficiency and human capital development—with diversity of thought and inclusion top of mind.

Scharrell's innovative model results in scalable and sustainable business success, leadership development and cultural transformation. Her intimate approach through vulnerability and poise translates into atypical windfalls growing organisations year over year at a rate of 25%, top-line revenue from 3.5M to 400M, retaining staff at a rate of 95%, head-count growth on average 5X, operational expense reduction over 25% and implementation of DEI and Great Place To Work transformation.

As the go-to DEI Specialist, Scharrell's ability to lead with diversity of thought while navigating the waters in industries lacking diversity, inclusion and belonging sets her apart. The return on investment in her leveraging obstacles into opportunities is immeasurable. She has a unique approach that motivates, inspires and captivates as a result of her offering prophetic insights, business acumen, connections with learning and tangible tools.

Scharrell has a proven track record of transforming one person at a time into a leader with a voice and a seat at the table while guiding individuals and organizations to outcomes that outpace the competition and create an ongoing legacy of high-performing leaders. As a keynote speaker, Scharrell's engaging and thought-provoking presentations leave audiences with actionable insights and practical tools that they can implement immediately to elevate their leadership to new heights.

WE ARE NEVER ALONE

CELIA MALAHLELA

I n today's times, where the world is all about glorifying itself, speaking about oneself and what we have achieved has become a normal behavior. In this picture, the world often only sees what we have achieved and seldom recognises the people who have played a role in our story. The truth is, without these people, the picture would not have quite turned out the way it has. I am African; ages ago my ancestors have recognized that personal development is dependent on the society around us. Society influences us. For better or for worse. In the olden days it was more for the better, for mutual support and growth. We call this *ubuntu.* I am because we are.

Allow me, dear reader, to tell you a bit about how in this very age ubuntu influenced my career and was personified when a Spanish woman also called Celia came into my life. But first, let me tell you a little about myself and what ubuntu means to me. I am a village girl from South Africa. Each year, I spend the Christmas break back home in the village reconnecting with my origins. The clean crisp air, the sound of the animals, the warmth, the fruits in the summer, the food over the festive season, people passing by as they stop to greet with so much joy. It is just irreplaceable. Sitting under the shade in my mother's yard as I write this chapter, I asked myself, *What does ubuntu exactly mean?* Having been raised in an African village, we are raised to have ubuntu. This is embedded in us. I speak Sepedi, the native language of the Bapedi Tribe from the North of South Africa. In my language ubuntu means botho. *Motho ke Motho ka Batho*, "I am because we are."

What better way to understand what the concept of botho really means than asking an elder? I called out to my mother sitting in the shade close by and asked her what she understood botho to be. The old lady is never short of words. Botho to us means being kind. It means doing things for the greater good and not for your own selfish interests. You would not walk past someone in need without lending a helping hand, let alone walk past someone without greeting them, whether you knew them or not. Most households in our villages were poor, but I can assure you, no one in the village slept with an empty stomach, she said. Growing up, I have seen botho all around me. I do not come from a rich family. My parents sacrificed a lot to ensure that they could send us to school. We did not consider ourselves poor and I do not recall looking at another household and considering them poor. I do, however, remember how our mothers used to borrow each other maize meal in buckets and sugar in enamel cups.

After I completed high school, I moved to Cape Town to further my studies. Occasionally I visited Pretoria during the school vacations. It almost felt like the further I moved away from the village, the less encounters I had with botho. When I moved to the city, I saw more people being rude, depressed, competitive, violent, there were homeless people in the streets, so much selfishness and even more sadness to say the least. In my language neighbors are called *baagishane*. Directly translated, this means "fellow builders". In the olden days, neighbors helped each other to build houses, plough the fields and raise kids. This is botho! Unfortunately, this is no longer the case. Neighbors do not even greet one another. It is all about individual survival, individual success, self-gratification, glorification.

I joined the defence and aerospace industry 2012. In this industry one rarely sees women in leadership or technical fields, let alone as owners of companies in the industry. I always found it remarkable when I spotted women in this industry. Even more so when I spot those that were in both technical roles and leadership. In November 2018, I came across a post by an organisation called WIIS.de (Women in International Security, Deutschland) on LinkedIn. A woman gave a talk about *"der digitale kampf gegen terrorismus"*, which is translated to "the digital fight against terrorism". Seeing a young woman in both a technical and leadership role was astonishing. It will come as no surprise that I quickly liked this post. Little did I know that I had just pushed a domino.

A short while after, the woman WIIS.de posted about contacted me. She thought my profile was interesting and it seemed we also had common interests, not to mention a common name. She wanted to connect with me and hoped to meet me in person. As you might have already figured, yes, her name is Celia too. Celia is a member of the management board and chief of strategy officer in a multinational hi-tech defense/security and aerospace company.

A few weeks later we met for breakfast. It was a beautiful morning, jacarandas were still in bloom and I can still remember the smell of the flowers and freshly cut grass at Irene Farm in Pretoria. We spoke about the industry, its challenges and so on. Halfway through she asked me if I would be interested to join the company she was working for. I was pleasantly surprised. A few months later, after several interviews and a strict selection process, I packed my bags and relocated to Europe, a place where I knew no one. I flew directly into the heart of a strong foreign culture and a foreign language.

They say one is born into a society and a way of thinking. Celia was born in Basque country in Spain in the seventies. Her parents were not from Basque country and could not speak Euskara, the native language of the Basque people. Basque country has a unique, strong culture, language and traditions which differ from the rest of Spain.

The independence of the Basque government was abolished in the early nineteenth century. Since then, they continued fighting for their independence. Nationalistic and terrorist groups were formed, conflict erupted, massive demonstrations took place and people were killed. Celia recalled that during her school days, she felt that she was living in a split society overshadowed by terrorism. At that point she was trying to convince the young people joining such movement that they did not have to be part of the conflict. She thought there is always a way of resolving a challenge without using violence. The reality is that we are not all the same. She never understood how anybody could think that separatism could be of benefit, but of course, that is a question of ideas and beliefs. Using violence as a tool? That is an absolute no-go in her opinion. She hoped everyone would come to their senses and live in harmony.

For one reason or another, like many teenagers, Celia could not wait to be independent. She felt she needed to be the best at school in order to give herself the better life she wished for. She left Spain for Germany when she was twenty-two years old. She wanted to prove to herself and the world that she can and that women can. It does not matter where you come from, if you are determined enough, you can. After completing her engineering studies in 2002, she joined the defence and aerospace industry. For any woman to be taken seriously in this industry, she would have to prove herself repeatedly from the first day on. However, when a man walks through the door, he is given respect, and it is already assumed that he is smart and capable to be standing where he is.

For the twenty years that followed, Celia worked hard to further her career, she progressed higher and higher in the organisation. From a project manager she developed into a board member of a multinational defence company, listed on the stock exchange. As a member of the management board and executive committee, Celia engaged with high-profile politicians, government officials and industry leaders from all around the world. She has experienced a fair share of marginalisation and misogyny. She cannot recall just how many times people assumed she was someone's secretary or the number of times she was ignored in the room. Some would even refuse to engage with her just because she is a woman. One can imagine how frustrating and painful that must have been.

Climbing a corporate ladder in any industry has challenges of its own. In male-dominated industries one must also navigate what I call "man-made hurdles". You are expected to compete in the race with boulders chained to your legs. You need to have a thick skin and be able to stand up for yourself if needs be. It is thus remarkable to find a woman who can climb this corporate ladder and advocate for others while remaining humble.

As disheartening and challenging as it is at times, Celia has set herself to show the world that it is possible. She challenges the stereotypes and questions things that the society tells us are impossible. Celia is convinced that we ought to disprove these irrational myths. We need to create a new normal, fitting to a reality where people around us as well as the following generations know that it is possible for women to succeed in industries we are in.

Celia does not claim to be an angel, a superhero or Mother Teresa. She is a normal person who believes she can contribute in making this world a better place, even if it can be just in a little way. She identifies what she calls little niches where she has a fighting chance to make and be the difference. She has established a think tank "Elevate" for the advancement of women in our organisation. Being in the role she is, in a company that is making a difference for a safer tomorrow, her contribution is already making a huge difference in the world. She is already making strides and making a mark for herself. It is amazing, that during the most critical time of her career, where she could be focusing solely on making it to the top, she is advocating for more women to come up as well. She is not in any way saying that women should be advanced merely because they are women. Capable, qualified women should not be overlooked because they are female. On the other hand, it would be irrational to promote women just because they are women. Decisions taken by leaders should be in the best interest of the company. Thus, we need to put the best people in the right positions, regardless of their gender. Celia is deeply convinced that we need to harness the power of diversity. Diverse thinking breeds unrivaled innovation. Over time, Elevate has evolved to address overall diversity in the organisation.

Celia wears her heart on her sleeve. She prides herself on being authentic and emotional. Some would say a bit too emotional and passionate at times. She is a hardworking, kind, authentic, transformational leader. Her energy is infectious. She is one of those people that you meet, and without even knowing who she is, you would know there was something special about her. She frequently says, "It doesn't cost anything to be kind. Just start with that. Help people where you can. Give a smile, you can never know who you meet and what they are going through. A little smile can brighten someone's day!" I am still struggling to wrap my mind around the pink fluffy poodle, Hello Kitty merchandise and pink feathers in her office. But that's her! She owns her truth, she is who she is. One can only perform at their best when they are themselves. This is how Celia connects with people and motivates them. She does sometimes wonder if the business world is ready for this. She believes that the success of anything is achieved by people.

As Dr Trent once said, "Women have a unique capacity to inspire, create and transform." This is because most women are not afraid to show their vulnerability and emotion. We are not afraid of our human side. We do not feel the pressure to appear as superheroes. Do not get me wrong, I have encountered men who possess these qualities as well, and I must say, they are great leaders. I have great respect for them, and some have also contributed significantly to my life and my career. Celia believes that you can only truly motivate people if you can connect with them, and you can only ever truly connect with people if you are genuine, that's how you inspire people to achieve objectives, reach for their dreams. Of course, when one is genuine and vulnerable, those around them will see that they are human. That they too also do fail at times.

The beauty of it all is that humans are indeed capable of great things. Celia is of the opinion that being authentic and vulnerable when it is needed is much more important than being the great person that never fails. That in itself doesn't relate to people, everybody fails. Everybody has doubts, some more than others. This way people around us will know that you can be human and still achieve great things. You don't have to be a superhero to be a leader in a multinational hi-tech defence and aerospace company. Of course, one must carry themselves in a professional manner without changing the essence of who they are. Be a professional human being, not a robot. Celia has reconciled herself to the fact that if being true to herself doesn't work out, then it doesn't work out. After all, you are the one that will have to live with the shadow you have created. And if you can find a way to live with that facade, or put it on and off when required, who am I to judge? It is your baggage to carry.

If only there was a manual to navigate this maze. Along the way I have found myself wondering if those who came before me also experienced the same hurdles. When one looks at the ones who have made it, one can hardly tell they were dealt a few blows along the way. All we see is the success they have achieved, who they have become. Similarly, when one looks at Celia, you can hardly tell she has had serious challenges of her own. Always elegantly dressed, cheerful and full of energy. Over time, I got to know that she has also gone through some of the challenges I have experienced, and this on its own gave me renewed hope on days that I felt like giving up, hope that it is doable.

Why do we do this to ourselves? Is it worth it? These are some of the thoughts that have gone through not only Celia's mind, but also the minds of many other businesswomen. The truth of the matter is that we need each other. Regardless of where one is on the corporate ladder, we all face challenges in one form or another. Without mellowing in our miseries or bragging, it is important that we share with each other the challenges we have faced and how we managed to navigate. Your story might help me overcome the hurdle in front of me. Sometimes it is just the knowing that you are not alone that keeps you going. We need to keep fighting to create the new normal. In this way the industry will get used to having people like us around and the generations to come will not have to run the race with these boulders chained to their legs. Giving up is not an option, she said.

Have you, dear reader, realised how we humans turn to fixate on problems and lose sight of all the wonderful things happening in our lives? I once asked Celia about challenges she has gone through in life. She said sometimes she looks at what is happening in the world right now and she would think she deserves a slap in the face for complaining about anything in her life. We all experience challenges. You can drama-tise it or you can say, "I am a gladiator and this is just a little battle and I will win in the end." Besides, if you give up without a fight, you will always wonder if tomorrow would have been a better day.

As you might have already gathered, Celia does not want to be remembered as a superhero. All she wishes for is that people she crossed paths with remember her as someone who tried to do right, some-one who was kind and good. I hope that this story will contribute towards making her wish a reality. That even people that have not met her would know about her. That she touched a lot of hearts, and most importantly, she did make a difference in this world. From one Celia to another, in the words of Maya Angelo, "People will forget what you said, people will forget what you did, but people will never forget how you made them feel."

Celia Malahlela

C elia Malahlela believes in being the change she would like to see in the world. She stands for international spirit, diversity and collaboration. She has a strong passion for universal humanitarian and social upliftment. Celia has served in non-executive director roles on several boards while still acting in operational leadership capacities in various organisations.

Amongst other qualifications she holds Master of Laws (LLM) and Master of Business Administration (MBA). Currently stationed in the European Union, Celia operates across multiple continents and cultures around the globe.

FINDING MY RHYTHM IN A WORLD OF SILENCE

ELISABETH GABAUER

As I write this chapter, my grandmother, who plays the main role in this story, has embarked on her great journey. She is in her dying process. I am with her, sitting next to her, holding her hand and watching her weak breathing. It's peaceful here; silence inherits the room. Sometimes silence is everything it takes.

All I can feel now is unconditional love, love from her to me and me to her. She is what I call ubuntu … and here is our story.

Since I can imagine I thought this world I was living in wasn't real, it felt like a movie, surreal to me. As a child I noticed a lot of people saying yes but their whole body was saying no or the other way around. Or I could feel that they wanted to say something but stayed silent. That was very irritating for me as a child because I always saw the truth—I think all children do this, and most of the time the people's inner truth isn't the truth they live and show.

I felt like a lost child in the wrong place. To me this world felt neither real nor safe.

What I felt did not match with what I perceived.

My mother was always very nice and courteous to everyone on the outside but I felt her emptiness and frustration inside of her. She was a very conformist woman, socially conformant. She never spoke for herself nor attended to her own needs.

I perceived my father as more real. He was very emotional but also more authentic.

Both were postwar generations and were just trying to survive, especially financially.

My mother's survival program was to control her feelings and needs, mostly with the help of psychotropic drugs and alcohol. My father worked well beyond his limits. I found him to be very hard and merciless towards himself and others. Because of their full-time stress and the bad circumstances they were in, they weren't able to really feel and see my brother and me. Now, I recognise that they had too much stress in their nervous systems to calm down and to reconnect with themselves and others, especially with their kids.

These were all circumstances that I only understood as an adult—as a child I just felt lost in a world of silence, lies and harmfulness. But I wasn't totally lost because my grandmother was there for me. She had the ability to see me. When I was with her, I felt safe and connected. I don't know why she was able to connect with me, despite growing up during the war, under the most difficult circumstances imaginable. She could feel and sense others in the most loving way. For me she was the only safe place in my family, although she was very socially conforming too. She played the social games, maybe that was her survival mechanism, but inside she had a very open mind and a big loving heart.

Although as a child I was able to see through the games people played, I soon acquired all the survival mechanisms that were shown to me—especially the "good" and "quiet girl" ones.

I was perfectly trained in being nice and got the most attention when I played the role of the people pleaser. This role was very easy for me, because I was able to feel how people really felt and so I constantly changed my behavior so that others felt comfortable with me.

I never spoke for myself. I was perfect at being silent. My wishes, dreams, longings and needs had to make space for the role of the good and nice girl.

This concept of life worked … until the real life awoke in me again.

It was the birth of my first daughter which opened my heart in such an intense way that I could feel life inside me again. It was as if my daughter, Viktoria, had breathed life into me.

Up until then I had functioned in a more or less socially acceptable way. I finished school, then I studied osteopathy, fell in love, built a nest and got married, just as it "should" be.

But the birth of my daughter changed everything.

I started to recognise the lies and silence I was living, the harmfulness and all the self-destruction. It was hard to look at my life honestly. It was one big lie.

Step by step I began to be more honest with myself, and step by step I had to face the consequences. One of those steps was my divorce from Viktoria's father. He was a good guy, but when I took a closer look at our world we had created, it was much too small for me. I wanted more from life, more than this secure state of being. He was supposedly happy in our little world, but I was very frustrated and living far below my potential. I could feel it so deep in my chest.

Everyone outside was shocked about our divorce because we were the perfect couple.

Only Grandma agreed with me. She said she had felt it long before and was just waiting for me to be brave enough to leave. During this she was my shoulder to lean on.

So I went into the world to find my true self.

But it wasn't so easy because all the survival mechanisms and roles I had learned continued to have an effect on me—most of them subconsciously. When I looked at my life, I was always able to feel my truth, but I was also able to ignore it in many ways. When you start to see your truth, you have to face a lot of pain. The pain of being a fake, of lost opportunities, of lost worth, living far below your potential and most of all to realise that you ended up in the wrong place.

All my life I had ended up in the wrong place.

Sometimes life can be tough but you know inside you are in the right place. Often when you have a goal sitting in the bottom of your heart, you'll have to face all your inner demons to reach it. This can be hard but you know it's for the greater good. Or you will have to face some stroke of fate, which is also hard but you'll know that's life and there will be better times.

But what I mean is to wake up and see all the self-taught lies you were living, maybe in your relationship or in your work or in a friendship. I've often tried to fit into something I never belonged in.

My work has always been an opportunity for me to live my authentic self. In my work I was able to express myself in the best way and let my creativity run freely.

In my relationships it was always difficult because my people pleaser program was running.

I was constantly suppressing and fighting myself to make my partners feel safe and be happy with me. My grandmother also had this program installed in her, but she was able to see it when it took possession of me, and thank God she was brave enough to tell me.

But most of the time I wasn't brave enough to look at myself honestly. For example, in the relationship after my divorce.

I had such a deep longing within me for a secure relationship that I did everything I could to ignore the red flags, to the point where I had physical manifestations of the problems. I couldn't sleep or eat, I felt nauseous all the time, but I held on. I tried to bend even more to avoid any conflict.

Yes, I had been through a divorce, and actually, I knew how it felt when I was no longer in the right place, but with this one relationship, I really wanted it to work, failure was not an option.

Two reasons were that I really wanted to offer my daughter a warm and tender family and that I believed that when relationships fell apart, I had failed.

I felt as though I was a huge failure.

My inner dialogue was screaming, *You are worthless, you are not able to be a good wife, a good mother, you will traumatize your daughter one more time …* and so on.

I ignored life in me again. I ignored that this relationship was very bad for me, this man wasn't a good man. He used me like jewelry, and I allowed it by suppressing everything that was alive in me. He used me to his advantage, everything he had promised me vanished the moment he felt he had me in the right place. I had trapped myself in a golden cage.

I had put everything into that relationship, all my money, my work (he became my business partner), my house, my time and all my beliefs. When I look back there were a few warning signs at the beginning, but I can tell you I was really blinded by love, or whatever you may call it.

After two years, after investing everything I had in the partnership, things got worse. Slowly it dawned on me that I was only being used as a cue ball. It was my grandmother who opened my eyes with only one statement: "Darling, you lost your shine!" and one question: "Are you happy in your relationship or are you missing something?"

I can tell you, I was missing a lot, and above all, I missed myself. I didn't like the woman I had become in the relationship and I didn't like my life anymore. It was time for a change.

When you realise that you are living something that is not your authentic self, then there is no going back, because from that point on you know you are cheating on yourself.

When this realisation arrives, it will become a really important cross-road in your life.

Life asks you inescapable questions: Who am I in the depth of my soul? What kind of person do I want to be? Can I keep my heart open even when it hurts? And how could I end up in this shitty place?

But how should I change my inner and outer world? And to be honest, I was afraid of losing everything—my money, my home, my clients and my social status—but thankfully the fear of continuing on the way I was, was greater.

And yes, I lost everything, he played bad games with me, but I felt strong with my grandma backing me up. She couldn't support me financially but she believed in me and she believed in life. Her belief in me made me move mountains, making things possible that seemed impossible and most of all she made me believe in myself.

I started from ground zero, and I started well.

Okay, I have to tell you, honestly, it was a real tough time, it really was not easy at all. Once I ran out of money to go grocery shopping, I told my daughter we were going on a potato diet for a week for better health—potatoes were all I had left.

Sometimes I prayed in bed at night that Viktoria's school wouldn't go on trips because I couldn't pay for them. I also couldn't pay the bill from the tax office either, but miraculously the woman from the tax office helped me and came up with some unusual solutions just for me.

I had the feeling that by giving space to life within me and telling my truth, everything would fall into place for me. Help came from every side in the most unusual ways.

My new clients brought me eggs and bread and cookies, my new neighbor helped me with my new home and my friends gave me things they no longer needed but would be of great help to me and Viktoria. Another friend helped me with social media to restart my business.

I was working very hard, sometimes seven days a week. It was not an easy time for Viktoria either, but my grandma was there for her. She helped us in any way possible, even though she also cared for my sick grandfather.

Sometimes when I had a new business idea or I was inspired to start something new, she always listened carefully, replying with, "Darling, if you can feel it deep in your heart, then I believe in it, even though you can't believe it yet. If you can feel it, I believe it! I know you can figure out everything." From my grandma I've learned that you only need someone who really believes in you and your dreams. Someone who trusts your inner life, even if you can't do it yourself.

I learned to focus on my beliefs and not on the beliefs others had about me. She told me, "It doesn't matter what others think of you, what matters is what you think of yourself. Are you happy with yourself? With your thoughts, your feelings and your beliefs? Do you follow the rhythm of your heart?"

My grandma was born before the Second World War, her father was killed in war when she was two years old. She was alone with her mum, without anything. As a child her stepfather treated her very badly and she never got enough to eat or drink. Hunger and humiliations were her daily demons.

At the age of seventeen she had to continue running her father's hotel, she was eighteen when she gave birth to my father and twenty when she lost her twins during birth.

You see, she had experienced a lot of bad things in her life but she never allowed herself to close her heart. She was silenced on the outside but she was able to break the silence in me.

Some weeks ago, she had a heart attack. She was resuscitated three times and operated on four times. Everything that could go wrong, went wrong.

But my grandmother's will to live was so strong that she managed to return home. She didn't want to die in hospital without seeing her great-grandchildren again, my two beautiful daughters. They weren't allowed to visit her in hospital because of the COVID-19 health measures, so she had to go home. There she was in need of care, but she was at home with her loved ones. This was the gift I could give to her. She always found the pleasure in having the people she loved around her. Now it was time to take care of her and to believe in the greater good, like she always did for me.

There were a lot of people in my life who helped me in difficult situations, a lot of people who helped me to become the woman I am now, but she was the person who believed in me the most. And for me this is the greatest gift someone can give to me ...

Grandma died in December of 2022. Now she is gone to another level of freedom and peace.

I know she is in the right place.

Elisabeth Gabauer

"When you find your own rhythm, life dances with you."

E lisabeth Gabauer is a body and soul therapist in Austria, located near Vienna. Her working tools are osteopathy, coaching, psychology and naikan. She has also been working as a birth doula for seventeen years.

Due to her family history, she was interested in psychotherapy and body therapy from a very early age. She has been practicing yoga and meditation ever since the age of sixteen, always fascinated by the connection between body and mind. The suffering of women in her family, especially the suffering and illness of her mother, brought her to the profession of therapy.

First of all osteopathy, because she loves the voice of the body. Elisabeth says, "Even if you can't speak for yourself, your body will do it for you." With the beginning of her therapeutic career, a great interest in spirituality came into her life. This curiosity led her to practicing Buddhist meditation, which is her daily basis of life and this preoccupation with meditation brought her to naikan. Naikan is her big love, the best way of bringing women closer to their essence. Naikan is a combination of Japanese psychotherapy and meditation. In a ten-day retreat you will be confronted with the three essential questions of life and thus find your way back to your inner self. You can read her story about naikan in the book *Naikan—Eintauchen ins Sein*. Working as a birth doula opened up the world of women and sisterhood to her. Elisabeth says, "During a birth you are very close to the source of life and the power of femininity." Her work with women is the work of her heart.

In Austria she gave birth to the "Weiberkraft Movement", now patented. This movement is a regular gathering of women in sisterhood to develop and support each other. She is also the founder of a podcast called *Frauencouch,* which gives women the possibility to tell their stories and empower others. Moreover, she accompanies women for twelve months in their personal development in her program "The Female Alchemy".

She is currently teaching naikan-based life and social counseling with her naikan mentor, Yoshin Franz Ritter, at the Naikan Institute and she teaches a new way of osteopathy based on spirituality. She has named this training "SoulTouch".

She also did a lot of training in systemic family therapy and trauma therapy. She is currently doing her master's degree at the Sigmund Freud University in Vienna. It's all about women's needs in a toxic society.

She calls herself "the beloved of life" because she knows that everything in life that happens to you, happens for you. It is just life's attempt to bring you to your essence. Sometimes life gets hard and narrow, only to give birth to a better version of yourself.

Who do you want to be? How do you want to live and feel? New choices give you new possibilities.

Her mission is to support women to overcome shame, blame, grief and guilt and to reconnect with their wonderful essence, to live a vibrant, joyful and pleased life.

Website: elisabethgabauer.at

BECOMING STRONG WOMEN, BECOMING PEACEMAKERS

BETTINA DANGANBARR & SARAH BLAKE

Together we rise.

In July 2004, fifty people from across Australia gathered at Dhudhupu, Galiwi'ku, Northern Territory. They were joined by Yolngu from across Arnhem Land and together were about to embark on a journey of peacemaking and leadership. Using mediation and ceremony as bridges, participants joined the Mawul Rom Project to learn what it meant to be leaders and peacemakers, to build bridges across cultures and empower a deep mutual respect.

From this place emerged many stories, but this is the story of two women learning to rise together as they embraced life and their purpose. But more importantly, it is a story of the women, cultures and space that kept them grounded.

Our stories intersected on the cliffs overlooking the ocean—bare feet, long skirts, sand in our toes. It was my second year and the first time for Bettina to attend Mawul, this is where we met as sisters—but it's just the beginning. The real magic happened earlier, it was a weaving of relationships, country and roles. It is magic that is still unfolding and growing.

HOW IT STARTED ...

When I started this journey, I was a young, somewhat naive white woman wanting to find her way and a desire to really understand more of Indigenous Australia. I was nervous, I didn't know anything, I didn't want to offend and I didn't know how to bridge the cultural gap. But I was really clear I didn't want to force a connection. I made a choice on that first day to lean into the discomfort with gentleness, patience and vulnerability.

During this first year, once all the formal learning was done, I'd sit quietly on the outskirts of the fire, listening and being present. I didn't have the language skills, but there was so many moments of shared understanding and laughter. My first real lesson—that we don't need a shared language to be able to connect on a human level. It was here that I met my Mukul Bapa (mother on father's side)—the woman who was to profoundly shape my understanding of leadership and the role of women in community. It was her who showed me the meaning of "together we rise".

Wanymuli adopted me into family—through my father's line. Over the course of ten years, I had the privilege to sit with and learn from my Mukul Bapa. Whether it was sitting by the campfire listening to stories, making and sharing tea or learning to make damper from her; together we struggled across the language barrier and emerged with a deep shared connection.

She gave me my place in Yolngu world, which identifies my relationships with people, animals, plants and land. She also gave me my Yolngu name, a connection to who I am and who I aspire to be. Over the years, she quietly guided me, held me and let me cry. She taught me about leadership, responsibility and grace.

My Mukul Bapa taught me how to bridge the culture and language barriers with love, laughter and patience. She was formidable too; I was both scared of her and awed by her. She embodied a silent power and authority, one look and I knew I had done wrong, but I also knew she would help me learn what I needed.

41

Over the course of that first week, we became family, this more than anything has shown me what it truly means to rise together. Not as one but as part of a whole—her and these strong women, who held families, communities and law together.

My Mukul Bapa and the other women held this quiet dignity and capacity to influence positive change their own way. A feminine leadership quality that was rooted to life, earth family and law. Strong yet moving where the wind guided them towards peaceful outcomes.

They laid the foundations for my yapa and me to step into our leadership power with humility and care.

Bettina: I remember when I was growing up when Wanymuli got older, her and her sisters together, I remember we used to go out hunting. And they used to teach us everything from plants, sky, animals, kinship, even though it was just like a camping or picnic trip. There was always that learning process—teaching and learning. I am very thankful for them that they allowed me to come with them.

These women taught me so much, and I admire their strength. I remember how close they were together; they used to do everything together. One wouldn't go hunting without the others. And we used to call them gomu girls; gomu means the hermit crab. And just like hermit crabs on the beach, always together, these women were together, and they were lifting us up, teaching us so much. They were cheeky, they laughed and they worked hard for their families.

I feel so lucky that I got to go with them, I sat down with them. They were always together, and I got to spend this time with them too, learning these qualities, all the manymuk (good/positive) about leadership skills or even just being, because they were very humble. These ladies were always approachable, teaching me about everything, and that's what gave me strength. So, when we are saying "on whose shoulders we stand", I know that it was them that gave me my strength, being able to love other people, see things from a different perspective because they always stopped to learn.

WEAVING STORIES

Bettina and I met in the second year of the project. I was working for the Australian Federal Police and Bettina was working for the Northern Territory Police.

On country, as we juggled multiple responsibilities from both of our cultural sides, we met. Nearly twenty years ago now, we two women, with such different stories and lives, discovered a shared relationship connection. Perhaps this is when our threads first entwined? It feels like it was meant to be, but like any real connection it has taken time to grow, bloom and flourish.

The careers for both Bettina and me have woven complex threads in a tapestry that is still being made. Life has often got in the way but like the shifting of the tide, our relationship has drifted in and out and our hearts soar when we have come back to each other. We have grown as daughters, mothers and partners. We have lived the highs and lows of life, persisting through deep grief with a sense of hope. Trying to maintain that balance of calm, grounded and practical.

We are learning to hold each other up but it is the women before us who taught us how to do this, they who have shown us how show leadership along our journey.

Throughout this time, we have both continued to walk and work in the conflict space. In different roles and positions we have focused on being the peacemakers and bridge-builders between our cultures, our professions and our relationships.

Bettina is an Aboriginal community police officer in East Arnhem Land. Her career has taken her across the territory as she has provided a bridge between western policing and Yolngu culture and law. She has also been on a journey of learning her culture and the responsibilities that come with that. This has included offering her home as a haven to dozens of domestic violence victims. In 2018, Bettina was awarded the Northern Territory Local Hero award for her work as an anti-domestic violence campaigner. As a vocal advocate for women in her community, she has pushed for change using both traditional mechanism and western structures.

This strong Yolngu woman is admired throughout her community as a peacemaker. A tireless campaigner for the rights of women, particularly those experiencing family violence, Bettina has championed the establishment of the Galiwin'ku Women's Space. This organisation is a community-led response that addresses family violence in a culturally appropriate, Yolngu-led way. Prior to this, Bettina operated a makeshift women's shelter in her own home, acting as a counselor and mediator to families and couples while also caring for her three children and two foster children.

As a vocal advocate for women in her community, she has pushed for change using both traditional mechanism and western structures. Bettina's expertise and knowledge working in two worlds—both the Yolngu and Balanda, or non-Indigenous—means she can provide culturally appropriate support and responses to conflict. She trains other police officers to understand Yolgnu culture. Her influence has prevented many crimes and supported many Yolgnu people as they move forward with their lives.

What Bettina has done is taken real experience and shaped it into something meaningful.

My own journey has been significantly shaped by my Mawul Rom experience. It solidified and brought clarity to what I wanted to do with my life—my vocation, to create spaces for those in conflict to better engage in problem-solving. So, my own career pathway since has been as mediator and strategist, and the things I am most proud of are the people whom I have empowered to be their own peacemaker heroes. It hasn't been an easy journey from working for the Federal Police, Northern Territory Department of Justice through to establishing my own company. But always I have striven to bring calm to conflict, to give people a moment to reflect and make wise decisions. In 2018 I also received the Peacemaker of the Year Award from Resolution Institute for work I had done with a remote Western Australian community. Perhaps 2018 marked a leadership turning point for both Bettina and me?

It was around this time that I made a conscious decision to step into leadership. I remember feeling so frustrated, by 1) having to clean up the mess from other mediators who would go out to communities with good intention and leave a trail of destruction and 2) hearing stories by these same individuals that failed to reflect the real mess left behind. Where were the stories of those doing the hard, gritty work? These people were too busy to share their stories because their focus was on delivering. I couldn't keep silent, and I couldn't keep waiting from someone else to fix things. My Mukul and the women from Galiwin'ku, they taught me more, and if I wasn't prepared to step up then I wouldn't have earnt my name.

These women gave me the confidence to elevate my own career, bring to the surface other people's voices and empower others experiencing conflict. But this is a long road I am walking, and it was only recently that I have been able to craft the next steps weaving together my conflict and dispute experience, and my passion for social and ethical issues in practical and meaningful way, launching a not-for-profit that provides remediation services for issues of modern slavery.

What we have both been able to do is lean into our vocational calling, our naming, in service of those experiencing conflict or the impact of violence. Our shared roles, whilst different, are also the same in that we hold people safely, helping them find their resolutions and hope.

Bettina: My time with Mukul and my time up there with Sarah, as a woman, a mediator and as a peacemaker has been so important. I learned to hold this space just to be and to give other people dignity to give them that space. And that wasn't a soft thing. I think that both Sarah and I do women's spaces well—we hold this space with such strength, and it's a precious thing. I don't think many people know what it is to hold this space. It is hard but also such a privilege.

I've been very privileged to be able to bring women together and empower them. Seeing all the ladies that come through the door, asking for help. You know, you see them at their lowest point in life, they feel hopeless. It's very humbling to just sit down with them, just give them that one or two minutes of your time. It might be a small amount of time but at least they see this hope.

LIFTING OTHERS UP

Walking in the conflict space is hard, and even harder when bridging cultural divides. There is so much pressure from both sides—power, influence and even undermining from those who see change as a threat. Too often we find ourselves walking a thin line—fairly providing support, strength and sometimes strong leadership. It requires a high level of self-reflection and discipline. A strategic, long view is needed to enable us to ask the right questions, both of ourselves and others. Perhaps more than most, we know the high costs that come when we get this balance wrong.

There is a real cost individually too. We know that conflict and violence is messy, people want us to pick sides, they want us to fan the fire of righteousness. There are obligations and responsibilities to manage and families to nurture. Often, we are pulled in many directions as mother, partner, other.

Nevertheless, we both push on with a drive to make a difference. As our weave continues to grow, we have both found ourselves taking on leadership roles not because we want status, but because we are deeply committed to finding ways for us all to walk together with calm, hope and dignity. This rising together is immensely harder than the blame game. This has meant that we have had to learn to negotiate and be vulnerable where others push through and over. At times we have had to "call out" our own cultural toxicity, other times we have had to bravely question systems, authority structures or call out for change.

I can't tell you the fear that sometimes pounds within, but for us both, our courage to speak, to stand up and hold the line, comes from our foundations. These foundations, the role models, are the women, the stories and the law that has helped to keep us grounded.

Bettina: My leadership, it came from all the mukuls. They were very important in my upbringing. Meeting you, and I think both of us, got our strength because we knew we were loved. I was supported. And I had good role models, and those women were our role models. We both, we were forged, we have gone through the flames and we have become stronger because of it.

We were forged through fire, it has given us strength and made us better able to walk this space. At times it has been hard, painful, confusing—we haven't always got it right, but we have pushed on.

We have both had to learn what it means to be a leader. Not in the traditional sense, but from a place of feminine authenticity. We have had to learn who we are; we have had to weather the storms; we have had to get clear on where we can make a difference and create strong boundaries around that so that we self-care. We don't always get this balancing act right, but we are both passionate about walking together.

But you must be grounded.

Bettina: With the police, with the work we both do in conflict and women in domestic violence, you and I must be grounded, we must look after ourselves. We must know ourselves. Because if we don't, we can't do this work. It takes too much, it hurts too much, so staying connected and grounded is so important.

Our ability to stay grounded through this messy work reflects on us. This is the story of our grounding, our "Muruwurri", our reminder to be strong. But the strength has to come from ourselves, from within. We need to be strong enough for ourselves to come out from that, and only then can we help others.

This is the story of the Muruwirri, Lathuwana, Gilkilmara, Ngaritjpal that Bettina told me:

"Out in the waters of the Arafura Sea, there is a rock, it is solid, strong, and whatever life throws at it, the waves, the storms and weather, this rock will always be there. This rock is known as 'Muruwirri'. This rock keeps us grounded, it's solid, it's embedded in the earth and reminds us to hold steady, to remain strong. But it also keeps us connected. As Djambarrpuyngu we have responsibility and are connected to this rock and each other."

The sharing of this story was a reminder for both of us. We are connected as family, but we are also connected to the earth, and it is this story of this rock that helps Bettina and me to stay strong when we walk in conflict spaces. It's our reminder. It is our grounding strength that helps us as leaders in our own way.

So, whilst we do "rise up together", we also know that to help others with grace, wisdom and strength, we also need to remain grounded. Being grounded is our ability to remain connected to our vocation, our purpose and our hope. It is that spiritual compass that lets us know we will be OK, that our purpose matters. It is this deep connection, like the strength of that rock, the "Muruwirri".

So, the women—the Gomu ladies, helped shape us, lifted us up by teaching us our foundations. These women taught us strength, foundations and hope. Perhaps most importantly, these powerhouse women, their presence helped us to know ourselves on a deeply spiritual and personal level and through that we seek to honor the responsibilities that come with that gift.

Betina: On whose shoulders with stand on?

Those woman strong courages women that cared and carried us through the flames.

The flames that forge us and creates a strong bond of love and strength, resilience and courage.

My mother is one of them, her totem is the Fire that burns beneath the water (Gurtha).

She has passed on her legacy onto me to speak up, be a leader and keep the fire burning.

I am here because of her and all my aunties that made the way for me to be leader for my people and bring unity and peace.

Mediation is like a small fresh water spring coming down and meeting the strong stormy ocean creating a balance and find a place to meet together in harmony.

Our flames never die even under the water of Nhalarang.

We stay grounded because of our continuing connections.

For both of us, in our own ways, we are seeking to be peacemakers. We listen and gently lift those experiencing conflict. But as leaders, we cannot be the strong calm presence for others if we don't be that for ourselves.

Being peacemakers isn't just about what you do for others, it is also about how you live that peace in your own daily life. Grounded and connected.

Bettina & Sarah

Bettina Danganbarr is an Aboriginal community police officer for the Northern Territory Police. She operates in East Arnhem Land and specifically the community of Galiwin'ku. Chair of the Galiwin'ku Women's Space, which she helped to establish, she is a tireless advocate for the rights of women, particularly those experiencing family violence. Bettina's expertise and knowledge working in two worlds—both the Yolngu and Balanda, or non-Indigenous—means she can provide culturally appropriate support and responses to conflict. She trains other police officers to understand Yolngu culture and works to help bridge the culture challenge.

Sarah Blake is an award-winning conflict strategist and mediator, TEDx speaker, best-selling author and media commentator. She elevates leaders, empowering them to overcome conflict barriers. Bringing clarity to complex decision-making during confusion, conflict and crisis, she helps transform problems into opportunities. With over twenty-six years of professional experience, Sarah has engaged in some of the most complex conflicts in Australia and beyond, and has worked across multiple industries and jurisdictions. Sarah has delivered talks across the world, both in person and online, and is considered a thought leader within the conflict resolution industry. This has enabled her to contribute to international advisory boards and support the development of the next generation of peacemakers. She is an accredited mediator with Resolution Institute and International Mediation Institute, is co-chair for Maat and the Australian ambassador for Mediate Guru.

A EULOGY TO MY MOTHER (AMAI)

CHIEDZA MALUNGA

A tribute to my mother, Tsindika Clara Maramba, who died in a road accident while commuting to work when I was three years old. A woman I have no recollection of and whose imprint of memories of the first three years of my life seemed to have gone with her. I owe my knowledge of her dear heart and brilliant mind to my father (Baba) and her older sister (Maiguru) who did their best to tell me about her. Little did my father know, after his death, the words he spoke to me about her would be the embers in my desire for an education. A desire to connect to a woman who birthed me and whom I do not remember, yet she is single-handedly the most important woman in my life.

Amai, my mother, a woman I am proud to be a descendant of. My mother grew up in Chirumanzu, a rural town in Masvingo Zimbabwe, and her hardworking nature and commitment to education in colonial Zimbabwe earned a scholarship post-independence to study midwifery in the UK. As I journeyed through my education, I have made life-long friends, including their families, who have provided wisdom and assistance in my journey. My point of connection with meaning and relationships, again, centres back to what Baba told me about her. My mother was a woman who had a deep love for learning. In my yearning to connect with what she loved I found a means to connect with others who have been my pillars as I journey through life.

Of all the inheritance that my mother left me, the greatest gift was her photos in various locations. Some in her homestead surrounded by the beautiful landscapes of Zimbabwe, some in her pristine white nursing uniform and some of her adventures of life as a student in the UK. Her photos are like seeing someone who looks exactly like me in a magazine that has no words but just beautiful pictures that I must create my own storyline for. But what those photos represent to me, are a portal of connection and are the foundation of my smile. I love smiling because whenever I look at her photos, her smile brings such joy to my heart. Whenever I see photos of myself smiling, I see my mother, the woman whose photos have inspired me to capture moments in my life and to remember to smile. Baba's description of my mother to me was, 'When you look in the mirror, you see her because you look exactly like her.' While I do not always see that, I connect with her photos as I go through various stages of my life. I am connected deeply to my motherland, I am passionate and connected to health equity and I love travel. Her photos left me with a legacy of memories that I connect with as I journey through life and define my identity as a black woman living in the diaspora. This woman I met, but whom my mind does not remember, inspires my heart, and the older I get the more I understand that I came out of her womb and went straight to stand on her shoulders.

Baba, I could easily talk about and write about for days, because I had twelve good years with him. Baba was and will always be my greatest supporter and the first person who taught me to work hard towards my goals and celebrate each milestone. He spoke to me about my mother, her love of gardening, her passion for education, her desire to create safer birthing practices which would result in a reduction of infant mortality rates and maternal deaths in post-colonial Zimbabwe.

When I was younger, I asked Baba why they chose Chiedza as my first name, as all my siblings use their English name as their first names. Baba explained to me that my mother named me Chiedza as she loved that the name means light, and for her, light closely aligned with revelation. Baba said she insisted that without light there is no revelation. The light for me was my education, and as I continued to learn and grow, the more I valued the work Baba put into ensuring that I knew about my mother. I stand on the shoulders of my dear Baba, in the knowledge I have of my mother. When I see my mother in my dreams, I feel connected to her and a part of her existence. I rarely dream of her but when I do, I feel sad. I feel the weight of my grief and how there are so many unspoken memories between us. When I awake post dreaming of her, I mourn the loss of this wonderful trailblazer who left a path for me to follow. Even though I have no memory of her yet, whenever anything great happens to me she is the first person I think of and miss.

My mother's older sister, Maiguru, was a phenomenal woman who spent a great deal of time ensuring that I knew my mother. When I gave birth to my daughter, Maiguru asked me to frame photos of my mother so that my daughter would know her grandmother and would continue passing on the legacy of this great woman so that she will never be forgotten. Maiguru's undying love for her little sister and the constant reminders to pass on the memory of her to my daughter through photographs is a shoulder I stand on. Maiguru, on whose shoulders I stand, never assumed the place of my mother even though she took up a lot of mentoring and guiding of me as I grew up. She taught me several life lessons and lessons on womanhood that I carry with me and use to anchor my experiences as I grow older. She taught me to respect and honour my mother and people's experiences and not judge them for their truth. She was a loving woman who committed her life to serving the community through a life of teaching and service. She lived most of her life in a convent, a life that a lot of people would make assumptions and judgements about, but she did not let that deter her from her purpose. She lived and worked in communities experiencing great vulnerability due to poverty, and her service and commitment to education and love for our people is an important life lesson I take from her. She believed and loved cups of tea, and told me countlessly that there is a brew for every ailment. When I was eleven, I sat with her and wrote out her life story as she wanted me to record her lived experience of the Zimbabwean Liberation Struggle as a young woman, and how her faith and knowledge of native plants carried her and the health of the women. She went through one of the most challenging times for young women in Zimbabwe's independence story. She is the woman who taught me to love a cup of tea and I have made connections and friendships and continue to do so with people over a freshly brewed pot of tea.

Photographs of my mother are my greatest inheritance and are my vantage point of the perspective of my mother. A perspective that I carry in my heart, that allows me to create and hold onto memories of a woman my daughter and I never met, yet carry in our hearts. My daughter loves my mother and her grandmother and always remarks about how much I resemble her. She misses her grandmother, and to her, my mother is very much an active part of her story. She is proud to be connected to her and speaks about her often as she learns about her ancestors. My daughter has lost both her maternal and paternal grandmothers, and yet she connects to these great women through lessons about our family tree and her ancestry. She enjoys hearing stories about their lives and weaves and connects those in her play and in her storytelling. Her paternal grandmother was a schoolteacher and my mother was a midwife, and in her imaginative play she has a school and a hospital that are run by female leaders named after her grandmothers. To live a life where my daughter and I look at my mother as an ancestor can be confusing, as she is technically not remote in the line of descent.

I lost this woman so early in my life that I connect with her existence more on a spiritual level than a memory-based interaction. I wish I remembered her touch, her smell, her smile and her hugs, but I do not. I do not remember anything, but what I do have are active memories of her based on the reflections I make from her photos. I have and continue to connect with my mother at various stages of my life and proudly stand squarely on the shoulders of my greatest ancestor, my mother.

My maternal grandmother, Mbuya Honde, was a loving woman with very warm hands. My memories of her when I visited her in the rural areas remain of her warm hands. She rarely spoke about my mother, but she did spend a lot of time holding my hands and gently massaging them. She would always encourage me to complete my chores speedily so that I could come and sit by her and get warm hand massages. My grandmother was a hardworking woman and instilled in all her daughters – my mother and myself included – a strong work ethic. Each time I visited my grandmother, her parting words to me were that working hard would open doors for me that even my parents could not open. I loved her soft voice and warm hands and when I was in primary school, I even chose her name, Mbuya Honde, as my nickname at home, and my siblings to this day will randomly remind me of that phase in my life.

One of my happy places is spending time in the garden, working on the soil and taking care of my plants. My father used to tell me that my mother would not buy vegetables but believed in eating what she grew in our garden. When I work in the garden my mind is still and my focus entirely shifts to the earth and its ability to nourish a seed to bearing fruit. In the same essence that Mother Earth provides life and nourishment, my connection with my mother provides me nourishment and comfort as I go through life and connect with different experiences. When I was younger, I used to run away from my gardening chores as there were more exciting things to do with my time, until my father allocated a portion of the family garden to my care and gave me the responsibility of growing sweet potatoes as they were one of my favorite foods. That is one of the most important life lessons that he gave me, as I was determined to ensure that I grew the sweet potato crop and when it was harvest time, I was so proud to display my bumper harvest. To this day, fire-ember-roasted sweet potatoes are one of my favorite foods. I attribute a lot of my love of the garden and learning about soil health and plant growth to my parents, and I appreciate that my father took time to talk to me about my mother and her love of the garden and that he ensured I found my own place to learn and engage with growing plants and taking care of them. I am passing on this profound knowledge to my daughter who is at the time of writing this, committed only to planting flowers for the bees and the butterflies and taking care of her mint plant as her gateway to gardening. My hope is that I pass onto my future generations a love of taking care of the earth and ensuring that they respect the connection of the soil to our health and wellbeing, a legacy my greatest ancestor left me.

A lot of people have played an integral role in my life and my anchor point has always been education and the different pathways it has led me to take. I am grateful that my parents, particularly my mother, believed in education and laid a durable foundation for me to be able to build on. I am grateful for the enduring friendships that I have made over the years in school, and now for the connections that I am making in the workplace and in other community engagement activities that I participate in. I am a grateful visitor, living in Naarm (Melbourne), and as I learn more about the culture of the Indigenous people of Australia, I am awed by the beautiful connections their culture and stories have to matriarchy. I am grateful that stories of great female leaders, mothers, sisters, aunties and daughters continue to weave through and interface with my experience in life, even as I live and visit in this great country. I love and miss my beautiful home Zimbabwe, and each time I visit my motherland, I am so grateful for the gift of belonging and connection with my history and my ancestry and most importantly to my mother. To my mother, Tsindika Clara, may your legacy continue for generations to come through my life, your grandchildren's lives as your story connects to that of other great women who have placed education a as an anchor in their life journey.

Chiedza Malunga

Chiedza Malunga is a public health professional with experience in refugee health and sexual and reproductive health promotion and research in multicultural communities. Chiedza has worked in statewide programs in Australia, ranging from individual and community-based programs through to policy and advocacy initiatives. She is passionate about building the capacity of individuals, communities and systems to respond effectively to the needs of the most vulnerable groups. In her current work in Australian health care, she is strongly guided by principles of equity and social justice to influence inclusive health care.

THE DREAM BEHIND
MY DREAM

LISA BENSON

"**I** 've read that book," I whispered to Mark, nudging my elbow against his upper arm.

We were snuggled up amongst the oversized cushions on the lounge at my favorite health retreat. My interest piqued as the Saturday night speaker—international best-selling author, Joanne Fedler—held up one of her books, *When Hungry, Eat*.

My eyes widened. I'd almost missed the talk. I was exhausted from the early morning tai chi, strenuous hike in the bush, as well as a couple of exercise classes. The evening activities *were* optional, after all.

"I might skip it and go to bed early," I said to Mark.

"But it's an author. Don't you want to write a book?"

"Oh. I didn't realize," I said, while mentally rearranging my plans.

As I sat in the theatre, I didn't imagine it being a life-changing moment. We are faced with dozens of seemingly insignificant decisions each day which direct the course of our life. The universe conspired so I would show up that evening.

As a young girl, I was fascinated with books, especially the emotionally evocative ones. E B White's *Charlotte's Web* was one of my favorites. I read the yellow-stained pages over and over. My heart swelled then broke as I followed the emotional journey of the characters. I dreamt of writing a book one day that would inspire others. My dream was innocent, unencumbered and naive. But I felt it. It seemed important and often hijacked my thoughts.

I connected with Joanne at the end of her presentation. I added my details to a contact sheet so she could notify me of upcoming workshops or writing retreats in Tuscany, Bali or Fiji. *Hmph … as if,* I scoffed. But a path was cleared for me and I felt compelled to follow it. Eighteen months later in 2016, I joined twelve extraordinary women at a writing retreat in Fiji, where my "real" book writing journey began.

Wananavu was 3,177 kilometeres away from home. Yes, I googled it one night towards the end of the week when I was feeling alone and far away. I managed a smile when my husband (fiancé at the time) Mark's name lit up my phone.

"How are you going, babe?"

"Yeah, I'm good," I said while trying not to cry.

"What's up?" His words were drawn out, probing for the truth.

"Yeah, I'm okay. It's just a lot harder than I thought." I paused for a moment. "I … I just feel like everyone is so much better at this than me." Then I let the tears go.

"Oh, babe. Isn't that why you're there? You're learning how to write. It's like any apprenticeship."

"I know, but we had to read out our writing today and I'm so embarrassed. Everyone read beautiful pieces from the heart and mine was so … superficial."

"I wish I was there to give you a hug."

"I know. I just want to come home. I don't think this is for me."

After we ended the call, I cried for hours. I wrote Joanne an email at 3am explaining my meltdown. I was relieved to admit, I was the one who needed to be here the most. It was the first time I realized I couldn't write a book on my own, I needed help. It was a humbling moment.

When I was younger I was afraid to ask for help. At school, if I didn't understand something, I'd wait until the bell rang to ask the teacher in private. I didn't want to appear silly in front of the class. The thought of my classmates laughing at me was debilitating.

I was also terrified of failing. The perfectionist in me never wanted to be judged, so I would sabotage myself or procrastinate to avoid criticism. I didn't know at the time that there are no failures and every mistake is an opportunity for growth.

When Joanne offered mentorships on the final day in Fiji, I asked her to hold a place for me. The truth was I intended to drop out once I returned home. I didn't feel ready, but a feeling deep in my stomach stopped me from canceling. My intuition was guiding me to step up, even though I felt a ton of resistance. Giving up wasn't what the universe had in store for me.

During those early months of being mentored by Joanne, I struggled. My writing wasn't flowing. I never heard the words she'd proclaimed to the others, "You've found your voice." *Will I ever hear those words?* I wondered. I must have found a terrific hiding place for mine.

As a lifelong people pleaser, my truth was concealed behind a false version of myself, the version I believed others would accept. My voice was clichéd and inconsistent. Like a chameleon, my words were influenced by my environment and the people I was interacting with. I wanted to have my say. I wanted to be heard. My voice was strangled because it was motivated by adverse energy.

Joanne saw through the facade and noticed I was trying too hard. I was writing the story I wanted to portray, not the one I needed to reveal—the truth. I had to get comfortable with myself before I could share my deepest shames and my greatest mistakes. Readers are proficient at recognising inauthenticity.

One day, Joanne offered a possible solution for my angst. "You could turn your book into fiction. It would allow you to be less restrained. You would have free rein to go crazy and not worry about what anyone else is thinking."

But there was an inner knowing—a calling—that I had tuned into. I cried at the thought of my story being fictionalized, a barometer of sorts.

"It has to be my truth. That's the whole point," I said to Mark while debriefing the mentoring session.

I started to comprehend how much work I had to do. Joanne's courses and guidance, the connections I'd made, the research and the podcasts I listened to, all helped me learn and grow.

Since my teenage years, I've been drawn to self-help and nonfiction books. I've read hundreds of them. The authors of these books have been silent mentors for me throughout my life and as I wrote my own book. I am thankful for the knowledge they imparted without even knowing it.

The women I met through Joanne's courses were a blessing. They taught me about myself and supported me, as I supported them. It was a community of like-minded women all lifting each other up and I have made many lifelong friends through these connections.

I learnt early on that it's impossible to write a memoir without mentioning one's mother. With no backstory or knowledge of where we've come from, our story is never complete. Mum spoke of her personal childhood experiences over the years, but I also interviewed her on several occasions with a specific focus on the themes of my book. Although it was emotional and painful to relive her childhood, she provided me with invaluable information about the family history and generational patterns of behavior. I am forever grateful to Mum for sharing her experiences and giving me her blessing to publish my book. Our stories are entangled, and by telling my story, I am not only standing on Mum's shoulders, but my ancestors' as well.

I heard Tony Robbins, American entrepreneur, author and business strategist, explain in one of his audio courses many years ago how babies cannot live without human touch. Parents produce chemicals for the purpose of loving their offspring no matter what, because without another human's love and devotion to care for them, they cannot survive.

Just as babies require human interaction for survival, I believe we continue to crave human connection throughout our lives. I have always wanted to belong to my family, within my circle of friends and amongst my work colleagues. I think many of us are fulfilled when we have a sense of belonging and feel we are contributing to our community. We can't grow in isolation. Just as flowers are pollinated by bees, humans feel alive when we are filled up by each other. Even as an introvert, I feel energised after spending time with like-minded family and friends who want the best for me.

For the following five years, I committed myself to completing my memoir. Joanne never gave up on me. She knew exactly what I needed to work through to become an author and was beside me through the difficult times as well as the celebratory moments—deciding on a title, finishing the first draft and finally finding my voice.

It wasn't until I took part in Joanne's *Sisterhood of the Rewrite* course in 2020 that I found my true writing voice. Sure, I'd written a lot of words, but the key to expressing my genuine voice was the enormous personal growth happening parallel to my writing. When I learned to be unaffected by other people's opinions through painful life experiences, my voice was free to emerge and the writing started to flow. I accepted myself and wasn't afraid to reveal my feelings because it no longer mattered if others didn't like me. I took full responsibility for my life and wasn't afraid to admit my mistakes. Previously I'd wanted everyone's approval. I had to be comfortable in my own skin and love myself. When I finally heard Joanne say those elusive words, I knew I was getting closer to my dream.

My clear and unrestrained voice was never going to appear until I had done the hard consciousness work. The writing, and all of the experiences

I had to go through as I wrote, were essential and transformational for my life as well as my writing.

I made an effort not to focus on publishing until I completed my manuscript. *One step at a time,* I kept telling myself. I didn't need another distraction or reason to procrastinate. Joanne introduced me to Karen McDermott, who had established several of her own publishing companies. I wrote an article for a magazine she produced in 2018 and we followed each other on social media for years but were yet to meet. I secretly wanted Karen to publish my book, but never thought it would be an option.

When Karen and I connected, our conversation flowed naturally. I felt wonderful energy from her, and a strong sense she was aligned with me and my story. Karen took me on as one of her KMD Books authors, and I have been blessed to work closely with her and witness her achieve magic in many areas of her life. Like Joanne, she is an inspiration. Another generous woman who supported me to achieve my dream.

When our dreams raise the energy of humanity as a collective, serendipity comes into play. Our dreams rarely become materialized in solitude. The right people turn up like angels to propel us forward when we are energetically aligned. It may be to give us confidence, to shine a light in the direction we need to go, or to provide knowledge or mentorship. Each piece of guidance I received was invaluable and perfectly timed. We cannot do life on our own. We are beings of community.

When I look back there was a string of connections essential for my book to be birthed into the world. My late nanna gifted me the funds to visit the health retreat where I met Mark. Mark prompted me to attend the presentation on a subsequent visit to the same retreat where I met Joanne. Joanne was my mentor and introduced me to many wonderful souls who assisted me, including Karen. And Karen guided me through the final stages to publication.

When we are on a high-vibrational frequency, we align with souls who assist us to accomplish our dreams. Life is a series of moments where—as if by magic—our tribe shows up. I have come to appreciate the synchronicity of life and how powerful we become when we work together for the betterment of humanity.

Joanne introduced me to the Kenneth Koch poem, *One Train May Hide Another*. It contains a beautiful message about being open to what is not obvious at first glance. It feels fitting to mention the sentiments of this poem here. The book I was writing was originally about my commuting days in the nineties, with a hint of my personal story. I ended up discarding the *safe* stories from my train traveling days. The deeper, vulnerable story was hiding behind that story—one story hid another.

Looking back, maybe my ultimate goal wasn't solely to write a book. I believe my book is the conduit to a greater dream. A dream to contribute to others, help them feel less alone and give them the confidence to follow their own dreams. Sometimes the universe puts smaller dreams in our path so we aren't overwhelmed by our ultimate purpose—one dream hid another.

Writing my book was a transformational journey. As I wrote, I began to heal. People who felt like obstacles turned up and temporarily stunted my progress or made me doubt myself. Difficult circumstances brought lessons to overcome before I could move forward. Now I see how every adversity projected me forward. My obstacles were my greatest teachers.

Who knows what's next? I know I am being gently guided in the right direction by many caring hands. Because I was surrounded by the right community, I was lifted, encouraged and supported. This, in turn, helped me gain the confidence to accomplish something I'd wanted to do for decades. It is uplifting witnessing beautiful souls holding out their hands to lift their sisters in achieving their dreams. The next part of my story, the dream behind my dream, will be revealed precisely when it is meant to be. My hope is every person tunes in to their intuition and follows the signs directing them to their purpose.

My experience in Fiji wasn't as clear-cut as I'd expected it to be. I'd taken sixteen thousand words to the writing retreat, hoping for a tick of approval. A gold star for my efforts as if I were back at school. I was confident my book would be published within a year. I chuckle now. Only one solitary line from that entire manuscript survived to live on in the final published version. If I would have known it would take five more years, I suspect I would have given up before I flew home. I now appreciate the journey I traveled was invaluable to my growth and self-discovery.

After writing a book, I read books differently. I no longer imagine the author sitting at their desk in isolation. I think about the multitude of encounters the author experienced to arrive at the moment where they were ready to share their words. This collective accomplishment is worthy of celebration and I have sincere gratitude for every person who has encouraged and supported me, especially Joanne, Karen, Mum and Mark, who have significantly contributed to me achieving this dream. The fact that I had to edit the acknowledgments from fifteen pages down to five, demonstrates how many people I recognise as making a contribution.

My childhood dream of writing a book wasn't a wild fantasy. It was the true calling of my heart speaking to me through intuition. The dream was inside me before I was influenced by ego. I hope the insights I gained from my journey to write my memoir, *Where Have I Been All My Life?—How I Finally Grew Up After a Life of Putting Up, Giving Up and Shutting Up*, inspire others to follow their own dreams. I want everyone to know they can accomplish whatever they desire, no matter how unreachable it seems. But we must have faith when it gets hard. Accomplishing long-term goals is meant to be challenging. There are meant to be obstacles on the way. They are our test to see how devoted we are to our dreams. But when we achieve them, the reward is deep fulfillment. The knowledge and skills we require appear when we push through even when it's painful or scary. If we are patient and dedicated, the positive forces behind our dreams will always be stronger than any obstacles we face.

We expand and transcend our consciousness when we breathe life into our connectedness. I would love to pay forward what I've learned, so others gain something from what I have received. Humanity to me is an endless cycle of giving and receiving. Never equal, but always in divine equilibrium.

Lisa Benson

Lisa Benson is a self-diagnosed recovering perfectionist who spent five years writing her award-winning memoir, *Where Have I Been All My Life?* During this time, she lived part-time on a boat on Sydney Harbour which she found to be a peaceful and inspirational space for her writing. Lisa and her husband continue to lead a "double life" traveling between Newcastle and Sydney each week.

Lisa has a Bachelor of Business with a major in tourism and marketing. She previously held various sales and marketing positions in hotels and resorts, and also worked in a real estate office. It wasn't until Lisa was in her forties that she decided to pursue her lifelong dream of becoming an author, and she now writes full-time.

Lisa's motto is Stop Trying—Start Being although she spent most of her life doing the exact opposite. Her writing is honest and relatable, and she hopes her vulnerability helps others feel less alone. Lisa would love to inspire women to stop wasting time living up to other people's expectations, to discover the magic of living an authentic life and to be free of self-imposed limitations.

Lisa Benson

Instagram: @lisabensonauthor
Facebook: Lisa Benson Author
LinkedIn: Lisa Benson

На чиїх плечах я стою[1]

BIANCA F STAWIARSKI

"Families are the compass that guides us. They are the inspiration to reach great heights and our comfort when we occasionally falter."—Brad Henry

As a Badimaya (Badimia) and Ukrainian woman, a visitor on Kaurna Country in South Australia, I sit and look out over the valley and think to myself about all the people I know who have contributed to my success. I sit in *ngardi guwanda*[2], thinking about life and how we so often celebrate people that are making enormous impacts and achieving incredible things in the public eye. But so often, we don't celebrate the unseen people, the people that help us get to this place, or even our ancestors who have gifted us with skills, strength, grounding and connection that enables us to achieve what we want to achieve or do the things that we want to do. This chapter is a celebration of the people who have supported me the most—amazing people that have contributed to my success in life over decades. Those people who have gifted me with skills, abilities and worldviews, determination and drive to arrive at this place in time. While this chapter is an honoring of all the people who have supported me, its focus is on the person who has had the biggest impact and is a form of *ngalimi yunguddya*[3] or Взаємність[4]. It is my attempt to

1 'On whose shoulders I stand' in Ukrainian. Pronounced na chyyikh plechakh ya stoyu
2 'Deep listening' in Badimaya / Badimia
3 'We give to each other' in Badimaya / Badimia
4 'Reciprocity' in Ukrainian

shine the light on this man and to give thanks. I could not have achieved or supported the people that I have without your contribution. In fact, it is likely that I would not be alive today without your intervention. Please see this humble writing as an honoring of you. To hold you in my heart further, I have used both languages important to me—Badimaya (Badimia) and Ukrainian—throughout this chapter.

КОЛИ МОЄ ЖИТТЯ ЗМІНИЛОСЯ[5]

I'd like to take you on a journey back in time, to a person and situations that seem almost foreign to me. I believe that there have been several pivotal points in my life, each one had the potential to completely derail my life and in one case, end it. Each of these circumstances brought me one step closer to placing me on the path of what I believe is my life's purpose. Through each of these situations one main person shone their light on me. This person held me, supported me and believed in me. It is also important to note that through these stories I want to make it clear that each person has their own journey. I have interwoven stories of pain, both mine and others, throughout this chapter, many of which have not been given voice. I have made peace with my struggles at different times in my life and I doubt I would be where I am without these experiences. So, I sit in the energy of *wiru*[6] and peer into the pain of my past, times that I rarely think about. I'll start with what stands out to me as the most pivotal point in my life, where I had sunk into my deepest depths of despair and fear. I ask that you hold this space in the way it is intended, which is simply one of awareness and curiosity, and of honoring of the incredible support networks that I have been able to draw upon.

I was overall a happy, confident, some would say gregarious child. When I was eighteen, I found myself in a difficult and abusive relationship. I didn't have the skills to navigate this, which culminated in an event one evening that changed my life. I will omit the specific details as I'm

5 'When my life changed' in Ukrainian
6 'Spirit' in Badimaya / Badimia

sure this situation is repeated all through our communities. One evening a former boyfriend broke into my home where I was alone. I'm sure you can imagine the ensuing argument and abuse that occurred that night. It culminated in me being cornered and crouched on my own bathroom floor attempting to somehow protect myself from his violence while using my body to also shield my dog from his attacks too. I felt trapped in the situation, with no way out. At one moment, my eighteen-year-old self did come up with a solution, a way out. I attempted suicide. Not my proudest moment, but in my mind at the time it seemed to be the only way to escape the violence. What was interesting was what occurred following this. The same person I couldn't get away from ceased his violence and reached out to the one person who has been my stabilising rock through my entire life, my father—Nicholas, or Mykola, as he is known in Ukrainian. It must have been incredibly hard for this young man to call my father in a situation like this, but I am grateful that he did. It also must have been beyond difficult for my father to receive that phone call in the middle of the night. To his testament, my dad was steadfast, supportive and calm. When I woke up the next morning feeling sick to my stomach, I was so thankful that I had survived. In that early morning, I was then able to see life as an amazing opportunity, a place of joy and beauty. It was as though I was seeing life through different eyes and I was so damn grateful that I had survived. I made a decision that morning, a vow to ancestors and the universe, that if I ever found myself in a feeling of being trapped again, I would draw on other strategies, find other ways to cope. Although I have been in abusive relationships since, I can honestly say that suicide has never been considered as an option since that time—and until that night it had never entered my mind either. After that night I have found myself in situations where I have been pretty scared, actually terrified at times, but I have worked hard to develop a better skill set and coping strategies as I matured. It's curious, but somehow my dad intuitively knew that smothering me, wrapping me up in cotton wool and watching me closely to see if I was safe following my attempt would have meant that I would have rebelled further. My dad treated me no differently to before my attempted suicide. He continued to model that quiet support and deep love, meeting me where I was. This formed the foundation to help me to repair my damaged wings and soar even higher than before. I will be forever grateful for his approach as I was able to heal on my own terms, regain my strength and build a tool kit that has continued to benefit myself, my family, my community and the important work I do in the space of complex trauma/decolonised mental health and wellbeing. That young woman seems to be a lifetime ago, and rather than dwell on that night and those circumstances, I want the focus of this writing to be about shining the light on my father—but before I do that, one more story of a pivotal time in my life.

Winding back my life to a much younger age, when I was eleven years old, I went to live with my dad and stepmother. My dad and mum had divorced when I was quite young and up until that time I lived with my mum, visiting my dad on alternate weekends. About a year after moving in with my dad, my mum left Adelaide and no one knew where she was. To my twelve-year-old self it felt like I was abandoned. I didn't know whether she was alive or dead, and I spent a long time deeply grieving the loss of her as my main childhood attachment figure. My adult self knows that my mum had her own healing journey to undertake, and her disappearance wasn't about me, although on the surface it may have looked like that. I recognise and understand this, continuing to love her still. During this time my dad, my rock, held me every night for about six months, wiping my tears and soothing me until I fell asleep. I slowly returned to balance over time and the tears lessened. Each time my mum unexpectedly called me on the phone, I was set back into my grieving pattern again. I remember my father angrily telling me that I needed to truthfully tell my mum that I wasn't doing OK, but each time she called I lied and said everything was fine as I didn't want her to feel sad. My dad is a quiet person, so that memory stays with me. Just touching into the pain and grief that my younger self felt still brings tears to my eyes. My heart is heavy as I write this, obviously still raw even though it was a very long time ago. As a mother myself, it breaks my heart to think about what my dad went through each night holding me until I cried myself to sleep. Yet each night, he would sit with me so that I wasn't alone in my grief. This continued until I felt strong enough to not need this extra support. That quiet strength and calm, loving presence greatly supported me during this time. Mya Robarts summed up my experience perfectly stating:

"The human touch is that little snippet of physical affection that brings a bit of comfort, support and kindness. It doesn't take much from the one who gives it but can make a huge difference in the one who receives it."
—Robarts, M. 2016.

My father's support, physical affection and love really did form the foundation of who I am today. This was especially crucial in my younger years.

МОЯ ОПОРА В ЖИТТІ[7]

This man, my rock, needs to be celebrated. My dad, a Ukrainian man, was born in 1948 in a displaced persons camp in Germany, in postwar Europe. His mother, father and his oldest siblings left Ukraine and travelled to Germany. His parents—my grandparents—were used as forced labor by the German government on farms. When my father was approximately one, his family secured an opportunity to come to Australia. They traveled from the displaced persons camp to Naples by train, then on the ship USAT *General W. G. Haan* and sailed to Australia, disembarking in Melbourne on February 21, 1950. None of his family spoke English. My баба[8] was illiterate as was common in those times in people from peasant farming backgrounds.

7 'My supporter in life' in Ukrainian
8 'Grandmother' in Ukrainian

My father struggled through life, in the early years living in migrant camps until his father built them a basic house from packing crates. He had to learn English and go through a schooling system that he describes as not really fitting him. He persevered and worked hard at a variety of jobs while attending school. Once he finished school, he obtained a position as a junior store man at a paper bag company. Being ambitious, he applied and was successful in securing a position as a laboratory assistant in a large government pathology laboratory. While he worked, he studied at night to improve his grades. After four years, his grades were high enough to attend university. During this time, he met my mother who had a young daughter at the time—my sister, Tania—and they married. Since my father excelled at his studies and as a laboratory assistant, he was offered a scholarship for his university degree. A few months before his final exams in a medical science degree, I was born. Bringing a child into the world during such an important and crucial time in his university studies must have been very difficult. Despite this, he successfully graduated, later completing a master's degree and spending the next forty-plus years working as a clinical biochemist.

My dad did some pretty amazing things all while ensuring I felt loved, heard and valued. He instilled in me a love of science, which is quite interesting because most people wouldn't automatically think of a science background when describing me. He also single-handedly quarried, selected and cut all the stone for not only my teenage home, but also the home that we currently live in. He has spent a lifetime caring for Peramangk and Kaurna Country, revegetating native trees where he lived and on the sides of the roads throughout the Adelaide Hills. He still hasn't stopped planting native trees! I drive past those roadside trees knowing that all those years ago he had the foresight to plant them. With my connection to Country so strongly felt, there is a deep resonance in this selfless act and the qualities he has fostered within me. It makes me reflect that poet, Wisdom Kwashie Mensah, was reminiscing about someone just like my dad when writing this:

"Our dreams come to light not because we're the luckiest or most blessed,
but the silent voices (voices out of the glare of the public) behind the scenes
helped show our light."

My dad has always been in the background of everything I do, supporting me, encouraging, in my younger years helping me with school assignments and attending my sporting events from time to time. He has been there at every low point in my life, crying with me, raging with me and quietly holding space while I focused on healing my broken heart. As I aged, went through my own university degrees, got married and had children, he has continued to be there for me. Unsurprisingly my dad became that steady, grounded and deeply loving support to my children as well. When I changed careers, entering the entrepreneurial space focusing on supporting women with lived experience of complex trauma, my dad commenced working just as hard in my social enterprise as I did. He is an avid reader of all my content, the first to purchase any books I have written, proofreads and edits all my book chapters, and along with our amazing farmhand, maintains and improves our sanctuary grounds. I have a twinkle in my eye that he will soon be reading this. So, Dad, thank you. From the deepest parts of my heart, I truly wouldn't be here without your support. I couldn't do what I do without you. I honor and value you for you and am absolutely grateful for your influence in my life.

Дякую тату. я тебе люблю[9]

BIBLIOGRAPHY

Robarts, M (2016) *The V Girl: a Coming of Age Story.* ISBN: 9780997203103

---

9 'Thank you, Dad. I love you' in Ukrainian

Bianca Stawiarski

Bianca Stawiarski is the founder and managing director of Warida Wholistic Wellness. She is a strong Badimaya (Badimia) and Ukrainian woman, who is a centered and purpose-driven healer, consultant, coach, speaker, lecturer, best-selling and international author, trainer and change-maker. Bianca infuses her calming, resilient, earthy, Indigenous connectedness into all that she does. As well as the work she does on Country, Bianca is sought out by organisations, companies and publications from across the globe. She is a certified mental health practitioner with an interest in supporting people who have experienced complex trauma, bringing the therapeutic space outside of four walls. She holds a master's in counseling practice, a diploma of life coaching, postgrad diploma of counseling, certificate in equine-assisted psychotherapy, a bachelor of Aboriginal studies and a diploma of contracting (government), amongst other qualifications. As part of her life's work, she is exploring *Ngardi Guwanda* (deep listening), Indigenous healing and lived experiences of plural communities. Bianca hopes that this can benefit some of our world's most disadvantaged and vulnerable people and provide a platform for people with lived experience to have their voices heard.

Bianca founded Warida Wholistic Wellness by recognising that communities needed something different to western clinical approaches to improve the growing mental health crisis around the world. She combined a clinical and relational approach of Indigenous healing practices together, outside on Country, facilitating a unique approach to healing needed in our communities. Whether that be working with Warida's horses through equine-assisted psychotherapy, taking a walk on Country with bush therapy, yarning circles or drawing upon the natural wisdom of the grandmother tree, Bianca works in an intuitive and integrative decolonised therapeutic approach. She is also a strong advocate for women in business and Indigenous businesses, volunteering her time to help them succeed. Warida Wholistic Wellness is Supply Nation certified and Social Traders certified Indigenous social enterprise operating at an international level.

Her work has been recognised over the years, with one recognition of note was winning the 2022 AusMumpreneur Awards in Wellness and Wellbeing GOLD, Women Will Change the World BRONZE, and Indigenous Business Excellence BRONZE. This has encouraged her to reach further afield, providing online services in transformational coaching, therapy, business support and personal development so that women have access to holistic specialist support regardless of where they live.

Bianca lives on Kaurna Country with her two amazing adult children, Savannah and Orson, her father, Nick, and a menagerie of four-legged family. In her spare time, Bianca competes internationally in horse archery.

Website: warida.com.au

RISING WITH GRATITUDE

KAREN MCDERMOTT

There have been many times in life where I have been elevated by others; they are an amazing blessing in my life, and I hope that I'm amazing in their lives in return. It's a beautiful thing be part of and it's something you must be open to. Whenever people ignite something within you or create an opportunity that you did not expect or think you were worthy of, but then you show up and confidently step into that, it's a very powerful part of your life and one that will carry the torch to inspire others.

I am a great believer in paying it forward, so all that I learn and receive I will share so that others can benefit. That's what we are supposed to do so that life continuously flows for humanity. The essence of that is simple and there is enough for us all, yet as a human race, we make it way more complicated.

For my first share I want to go back to my childhood. I was very blessed to be allowed to be curious and experience life. Yes, I was told what was right and what was wrong, but generally I was pretty good. I didn't love school; I attended a convent grammar school that did not hold my interest in class. I didn't "get it".

Interestingly, it was a year when the entrance exam for the higher-end schools was changed, and after attending three months at a regular secondary school where I was top of the class, I was awarded a scholarship to a convent grammar school where I joined after others had established friend groups, soI felt somewhat behind. I just never got the way that only the elite were focused on and the rest ignored as if they were invisible.

I went into work as soon as I left school. Then I became a teenage mom at eighteen. Being a mom was the most beautiful thing, and I feel very blessed to have never needed to make a choice between having and not having my baby. There were so many girls when I was growing up in Ireland, even recently, I heard of young girls who got pregnant and their parents would either send them off to a convent or take them to get rid of the child, thinking that it would ruin their life. And yet my son being born and me being a teenage mom was one of the best things that ever happened to me. I really and truly feel very blessed that my mother was there at that time.

I remember at that time, your a family would have a lot of shame because of this. But my mother said that everything would be fine, that new life is beautiful—and to have that in your heart and know that everything would be all right whenever something's pretty scary is a beautiful thing. And so as soon as they're born, there's never any shame, they're there and you'd never change it for the world—nobody would. I never took this for granted ever. My mom has gifted me many wisdoms during my life, many of which I didn't acknowledge at the time, never stopping me even when it was a big change in her life as well as mine.

And whenever I would face a life challenge and come to my mom with a worry, she would simply state, "Just do what makes you happy, that's where the answer is."

It's such a simple statement and yet so profound that it has always stayed with me. I realise that as humans we make life so complicated and when we find ourselves at a crossroad, of which we will come upon many in our lives, we simply need to navigate the path that brings us joy. My mother sharing with me this insight has gifted me permission in life to pursue what makes my heart sing without any guilt, but instead a knowing that if I am happy others around me will benefit. I believe it is a simple yet powerful essence of the magic of life.

New life is the most beautiful thing in the world. My mom was a mother to six and in turn I too found myself a muom to six. Being a teenage mom and being supported in that was beautiful. I believe that there is no coincidence in that. Even though I didn't intentionally set out to have six children, I knew that when I had my sixth that was it.

I am made of different things than my mom, she was so content being at home, reading and being there for us supporting our dreams and ambitions. Through her encouragement, I am the ambitious mom who is home-based but building a publishing empire because I discovered the power in stories. I have a fearless approach to it all because I navigate through a powerful knowing.

The second most poignant time that comes to mind was shorty after I emigrated to Australia. When I arrived here thirty-five weeks pregnant with my third child. I was engulfed with so much creativity. I expressed it initially through writing and illustrating homemade children's books with my kids. Then one day, my limiting belief about writing was shattered by a very dear friend, Donna, when she opened my mind to the possibility of being able to write fifty thousand words. And little did I know it opened my awareness; it opened my belief in myself. And little did I know that within a few days I was going to have an epiphany about the double miscarriage I had endured before I got pregnant with my third child a few years previously. That epiphany would gift me the answer my heart longed for, the answer no medical doctor could give but instead a spiritual answer that would gift me peace and a passion to share it with he world through story.

A few days later, I became very aware that I was to write a book about it. Now, writing a book whilst I just had my fourth child was not ideal timing, but yet the call was loud, I couldn't ignore it and to be honest I didn't want to. Remember I said I was ambitious! The interesting thing was that I had never been good at English at school, I had a teacher who made me feel bad and uneducated about words. But with my renewed belief I understood that stories have to be written and that they can then be made universally legible afterwards. My next step was to write. So when NaNoWriMo was introduced to me two days before it was to start, I accepted the challenge. I managed the expectations of my family by telling my husband he did not have a wife for thirty days because I was going to write a novel, and that meant 1,667 words a day. I would love and nurture our children but everything else would be limited for the month of November. *The Visitor* was born that month, and little did I know that that was only part of the journey. It was the next step, and it was going to be a catalyst to so much more.

You see, had I known what was to come, I may have been overwhelmed and not followed through. That is why it is important to honor the very next step and that you have the courage to step forward towards each step, and before you know it you have journeyed so far towards your dreams.

Now, on whose shoulders I stood for that, I stood on my own, but leaned on support around me to make it happen.

When we show up through our wisdoms and share, a sort of yellow brick road appears and when we wear our ruby slippers and dance our way along the path, magic awaits!

The third time I would like to highlight is when I attended the 2015 AusMumpreneur conference. I couldn't afford to go and was gifted a scholarship to attend. What I learned at that event would change my life. The two women who host that event are Peace Mitchell and Katy Garner, and if it were not for them I would not be where I am today! They bring amazing humans together from startups to billion-dollar company founders because they know the power of what happens when those who succeed share their stories and what it ignites in someone else. It truly worked for me and every year I have an AusMumpreneur success story to share and I absolutely hope that I have paid it forward back into this amazing community that impacts so widely.

It was because of attending this first conference that I realised I was playing too small and safe and that I needed to do something innovative to get visible. I set the intention and an inspired thought hit me, that I should reach out to a castle owner when back in Ireland visiting my family to see if he would like to host a writers' retreat. I had this huge sense of knowing this was the next step and when he said yes it was a perfect fit, I booked it. Not knowing if anyone would come but they did, and in March 2017 we hosted our first Serenity Press Writers' Retreat at Crom Castle, Northern Ireland.

And it all began with that first step of having the courage to show up in a beautiful community of like-minded people that elevate. I just honored a journey to share stories, and it has brought me on an epic adventure, one where I get to make wonderful things happen for others and for myself.

And a final time that I would like to share is when I reached out to Sarah, Duchess of York, to see if she would like to publish a children's book with Serenity Press. Many people ask me how that happened and it went something like this … I was watching a Facebook Live late one night where the Duchess was speaking at an event in London, and my train of thought was, *Oh there is Sarah, Duchess of York, she used to have* Budgie the Little Helicopter, *my son loved him, I wonder if she would like to do a book with Serenity Press*. I took immediate action by googling who her agent was and I wrote them what must have been the best email and two weeks later the Duchess' business manager reached out to chat. We ended up on a call at the most inconvenient time for me as a mumpreneur as I was on holidays with five of my children in Bunbury and the full day was geared to my hyperactive youngest being asleep at the time of the call but when they messaged to ask if we could do the call forty-five minutes earlier I surrendered to the notion that there was going to be background noise and showed up anyway. It ended up being a positive because they got to know me from the very beginning. Yes, I am a mum in business, my kids do come first but I still show up. That was in 2019, and in 2022, we set our own division that has recently been turned into our own company.

These are a few of the most poignant times in my life that came up for me when writing this chapter. There are of course many people in my life who I have leaned on and do so regularly, my eldest son works with me, I couldn't do what I do without him. My sister Emma and I are so close, we talk most mornings and raise each other up all the time, and I have wonderful friends who I can lean on when needed and they can do the same with me.

I believe that life is a series of giving and receiving, we must surrender and allow it to flow because the receiving is just as important as the giving. There is no shame in it, there is only ever wonderful things that come from accepting the hand of someone else who will lift you on to their shoulders and elevate you. Our job is to be grateful, make the most of the opportunity and share the experience with others. Wouldn't our world be the most amazing place if everyone threw their egos aside and honored this process!

I hope that by reading my experiences that you can now identify times in your life when you were elevated by someone else and that gratitude beams from you to attract more of the same for you and others.

Karen McDermott

K aren is an award-winning publisher, author, TEDx speaker, and advanced law of attraction practitioner.

Author of numerous books across many genres – fiction, motivational, children's, and journals – she chooses to lead the way in her authorship generously sharing her philosophies through her writing.

Karen is also a sought-after speaker who shares her knowledge and wisdom on building publishing empires, establishing yourself as a successful author-publisher, and book writing.

Having built a highly successful publishing business from scratch, signing major authors, writing over thirty books herself, and establishing her own credible brand in the market, Karen has developed strategies and techniques based on tapping into the power of knowing to create your dreams.

Karen is a gifted teacher who inspires others to make magic happen in their lives through her seven life principles that have been integral in her success.

Ubuntu

When time and circumstance align, magic happens.

Website: kmdbooks.com / serenitypress.org / mmhpress.com

WHERE YOU NEED TO BE

MARGARET WILLIAMS

T he sun had not long risen over craggy Moffat Headland. Seagulls were swooping over the clear water, looking for a morning fish delight. The ocean was sparkling with tiny points of solar light. My grandfather had roused me up with his wake-up whistle, which he always managed to perform with a cheeky smile. Along with the whistle came a panican of milky tea and a piece of buttered bread with sugar sprinkled on it. This was a daily ritual of his.

Today was THE DAY: the day he would take me out in the waves, out of my depth! I would soon be starting school and was therefore "big enough" for this adventure. I was bursting with excitement, bubbles bursting in my heart, my tummy and anywhere else there was room for them.

Holding my grandfather's hand as we walked together down the sandy path to the beach, he spoke softly about what a wonderful world God had made. He pointed out native flora and named birds as we traveled along. On reaching the beach, we sat on our towels on the sand for a few minutes and he told me he knew I was grown up enough for this adventure. I had in the present moment every resource of positive energy I needed. Today, I can close my eyes and experience that morning with delight.

A whisper of love, a silken strand,

A tapestry begins in a life unplanned.

When we were waist deep in water, he took me gently in his arms, smiling eyes looking into mine. Oh, the feeling of safety was enormous! Over the waves we floated together for quite some time, and then he fixed his gaze upon me and said, "Wendy, fight the waves and you might drown. Go with them and they'll take you where you need to be." Then he released me. Something inside me responded to the implicit trust I had in him. I relaxed into the waves and where I needed to be was the sandy shore, firm beneath my feet! Leaping with joy, I quickly found his broad smile. I ran through the water back into his arms to repeat the process many, many times, until he called it a day. I think I could have gone on forever!

Those wise words have never left me. The brain is an adaptive and malleable organ which senses, processes, perceives, creates memories and acts on information from the internal and external environment. The words embedded in my subconscious. Indeed, perhaps they tattooed themselves on my brain! They have guided me, becoming, I believe, my mantra.

The flip side of the narrative is the trust he had in me. I was a spontaneous child who was probably unpredictable. Yet he knew we shared an indefinable bond and must have been sure I would listen to him. I say this because years later I learned that he could not swim and therefore could not have saved me!

When I ponder on this, I feel overwhelmed with gratitude that my young life was blessed with such a gentle, mentoring presence. Wherever I have lived in the world, this feeling of comfort and security has remained in my spirit. The waves symbolise my life journey, a progressive motion, sometimes gentle, sometimes swirling and rough, yet guiding my search for authenticity and meaning. The beach represents the environment in which I find myself. The context is the mantra that the waves have taken me where I need to be.

Yet there is another picture I must share from that morning.

In a little sandy nook at the bottom of the headland sat another part of me, watching this enchanting interaction.

"How can a part of you be swimming and part of you be watching?" you might understandably ask. Let me explain:

The day before this magical day had been a strong contrast. My mother had told me some stunning news. When I went to school, my name would not be Wendy anymore. It would be Margaret.

"Why?" I said.

"Because you will never fly," she responded.

I had no idea what she was talking about and thought, *Why would I need to fly?* I went off to play and as my mind was firmly fixed on my big-girl swim the next morning, I let it go.

However, Wendy had no intention of disappearing into retirement! She has been with me ever since, free from the concepts of space and time, guiding me, sharing her unique wisdom. Her power of observation and her freedom to "be wherever she needs to be", offers a fluidity to my life which is soothing, sometimes surprising, yet always loving. She is unrestricted and can certainly fly.

These were two life-changing days for me, though a little five-year-old had no cognisance of how important they were. In altering my name, my mother tampered with my earthly identity. Yet, the eternal flow of life has a way of balancing changing aspects. My grandfather's words that day imprinted themselves on every part of my being and nourished my spiritual identity. As my life has unfolded, I have applied his wisdom repeatedly. He not only held my hand and cradled me in his arms. He invited me to stand on his shoulders. He lived ubuntu … and he enabled Wendy and Margaret to live ubuntu as well.

Perhaps I should explain more about my name change. My mother's first child, a girl, was stillborn. My mother fought the waves of grief and was drowning in her own tears. She never said anything more than the fact she had lost her baby. I, her next female child, was drowning in the water of her cries. She envisaged her first little girl as an angel, so she named me Wendy after the character in *Peter and Wendy* by J M Barrie. Wendy could fly like an angel.

I have always been a person who thinks outside the box, often to the dismay of those who share my life. In fact, I had a dear friend who called me "The Comet", as he said, "Wow! Where did that come from?" My behavior sometimes manifested that outside-the-box thinking, a trait my mother found difficult. Obviously, I was not shaping up to be her angel, so she decided to change my name. I discovered all this many years later through an unfolding of the secret when the time was right. I was where I needed to be.

As a counseling teacher, I used my genogram one day to illustrate record keeping. One of my students asked me if I would like her to have a service and "give my sister to God". With my permission, she had the dedication. The next time I spoke to my mother on the phone, on Mothers' Day, she asked me if she could talk to me about her first baby, something she had never done before! She talked honestly at length about this part of her life, weeping amidst the tragic story which was unfolding. I was able to be there with compassion and love. She said that the hardest part was she had never been able to hold her little girl or have a funeral for her and there was no record that she had ever existed. At the end of our conversation, she told me she loved me, the only time in my life I ever heard those words. This liberation for my mother cannot be explained in a lineal perspective. It was a quantum shift in the metaphysical for us both.

A whisper of love, release of tears,
Beauty restored after so many years.

My mother never mentioned that conversation again. I had bought her a beautiful plant, for my sister, and she would talk at length about the plant. Upon her death, I was able to take the opportunity to complete her journey. On her death certificate, I could name my sister and give her an earthly record of her reality. Ah, the wonder of synchronicity!

When I started school as Margaret, I was often chastised for not responding when my name was called. I quickly learnt. I became skilled at enhancing the life I led as an adaptive "human doing" and a separate, often private, "human being". My being center, my essential self, had an irresistible compulsion to become who I really am, just as every organism is driven to assume the form that is characteristic of its nature, regardless of the environment. I responded to this central energy, always wanting to KNOW how, what, where and why. One of my enduring memorandums is "I don't know how NOT to know". I have maintained a thirst for knowledge, for understanding, for meaning. I reflect on information and contemplate on the reflection.

To illustrate this, I want to digress over many decades to share a recent view from my grandfather's shoulders. Two years ago, I was diagnosed with melanoma in my liver and lungs. The hospital was locked down because of COVID-19. So, I was all alone to ponder a life-threatening illness in a system where data is of primary importance and compassion is now virtually absent. Instead of fighting the waves of fear and sadness, I went with them. After all our human generator is powered by our e-motion—energy in motion—and I certainly needed to move from the abruptness of the diagnosis. Fear is a sharp energy and I used that to keep me firmly in the present. The sadness gave me a blue pool of quiet in which to rest. In a brief time, an awesome sense of calm surrounded me and has been with me ever since.

I was discharged from hospital, and where I needed to be was meditating on our veranda, where the bush environment envelops me. My very being responds with joy to the sight, the smell and the sounds of nature. The answers emerged in fascinating sequence and from unexpected people: an ancient indigenous medicine named gumbi gumbi, a hypnotherapist who is very skillful and an oncologist who listens and could prescribe infusions of a protein which will hopefully melt the melanoma's protective shield. So here I am, still living and loving life! I have gratitude beyond belief.

Wendy has been very present since that diagnosis, providing me with memories which need reconsideration from my grandfather's shoulders. I had a dream where I came across a web with little pieces of a shattered mirror stuck to it. A heavy rainstorm came, washing all the fragments off. I frantically tried to pick them all up, but I could not. Then I realised that they did not belong to me, so I stood and watched the water wash them all away. The web was then shimmering and clean and I didn't know what to do with it. A voice said, "It is just gossamer. Wrap yourself up in it, rest and be still."

I really resonate with the words, "Be still." Often in that stillness, I become at one with my environment and feel formless. It is a beautiful sensation.

Yet, there have been times in my life when I have succumbed to fighting the waves. One of these was the heartbreak of being shunned by my immediate family of origin over a moral issue. My despair was profound. I almost drowned in that one, floundering in confusion, suffocating in the silence, flailing in their apparent lack of justice. I could only bootstrap myself out of those deep waters through the view and wisdom from my grandfather's trusted shoulders—*Be what you most need.*

I asked my grandfather once about his deep, simple faith. He freely shared his spiritual beliefs, and how important it was to be strong and firm in a world which was often difficult. When I asked how to do that, his answer was very clear, 'Be your faith, believe your truth and stand by it. Live your faith, Margaret.'

So, over many years, I honored my emotions, cried rivers of tears, but offered love to them in my heart, mind and soul. It was an arduous journey, requiring constant attention and courage. But it was worth it! As a result, I was able to farewell my mother with affection and respect. The agonising hurt had been absorbed by the very love which is circular. The love we give out returns to us in abundance. This may be from surprising aspects, but why should we be surprised? Love simply is, not franchised or confined, as our earthly existence would envisage it. Love resonates in and through the whole of creation.

It is interesting that one's genetic family of origin can be the source of such inspiration and such pain—the alpha and the omega of human life as we know it. As I see it now, our genetic selves are simply a way of existing on this earth. Our spiritual selves are our essential selves. Wendy, long ago, knew this different paradigm: being an essential microcosm in the eternal flow of the universe, free from all the restrictions we humans place on ourselves. Wendy freely offers her metaphorical shoulders, perhaps her wings, to offer me a transcendent view of my life.

That life has indeed been a varied, exciting, challenging and blessed one when I look at it from Wendy's view. There have been constant threads in the tapestry, one of which is being in touch with the earth, gardening in whatever form I was able, even if it was just a couple of little pot plants! Where did I learn about this craft that has become a passion? From my grandfather!

He was a farmer who somewhat reluctantly became a politician. So when his work forced him to live in the city, he bought twenty-five acres of land so he could remain in touch with his passion. He lived largely subsistently, had beautiful flower gardens and even a donkey. I remember him taking me by the hand to collect the eggs for us to eat and the chook manure for the vegetable seedlings to eat! I had little blonde plaits and one day a rooster jumped up and pecked the end of one of them. I screamed … but my grandfather said, "That's a rough hello. Are you going to say hello back?" Respect for all, even the rough rooster! Another lesson learned.

The ability of the earth to absorb tension is remarkable. I am not sure whether I was born with an embedded knowing or whether Wendy nudged me, but I knew this as a young girl. After my father returned from the Second World War, he became an alcoholic. Thus, there were times when our home was an unhappy, and sometimes unsafe, one. I developed a strong need to protect my younger siblings. Somehow, I knew to creep down the back stairs and lie flat on my back on the grass to relieve this tension. I would look up at the clouds and make up little stories about them. My God lived in those clouds, and I could climb in a soft, safe place and smile. My garden has always offered me the same balm, even to this day (and I still love clouds!).

A whisper of love, a garden unfolds.
Balm for the heart, food for the soul.

Having a garden enhances our ability to share. A bunch of flowers, some cuttings we have been able to propagate, some seeds gathered or some nutritious vegetables and fruit, all enable us to perform random acts of kindness. They are often conversation openers. I have always made a practice of giving family members a living plant for their birthday. It's a gift which symbolises life and goes on giving.

When I had my counseling practice, I was often reimbursed, not with money, but with plants or home-baked goods. In this way, I could offer my skills to a broad range of people. My grandfather, as in fact did many family members, volunteered in community organisations their whole lives. That spirit of giving oneself in whatever way possible was a great role model to follow.

Another thread revolves around rising to an occasion. My grandfather was known in political circles as "The Gentleman". He conducted his life with dignity and lead by example. He had a keen sense of humor and he held no grudges. In my last year of school, after an induction service of school leaders, he simply fixed his compelling blue eyes upon me and said, "Lead well, Margaret." No advice or instructions followed. Again, he had implicit trust that I had all I needed to fulfill the calling.

Having all we need was a thread from his tapestry. He would quote the verse from Matthew 6:26–27: "Be not anxious for your life ... Consider the lilies of the field, how they grow, they toil not, neither do they spin ..." He taught me to be grateful, to be mindful, to invest myself in a beautiful existence instead of physical vanity. In solving a problem, he educated me to look for the answer in what I already possessed or knew first, before looking for an external solution.

A whisper of love, wisdom flows,
Listen intently, the mentor knows.

I have been blessed with many mentors throughout my life—people who could see the real me, who encouraged me to fulfill my potential, who respected me enough to challenge me, but most of all, who offered me love. From those trusted shoulders, and a little nudge from Wendy, I was able to recognise these wonderful people, to engage with them, to listen to them, to develop the skill of applying knowledge so it could become wisdom. They supported me, confronted me and walked with me through some wonderful and some difficult times, for which I am eternally grateful.

The giving and receiving of unconditional love, as I understand it, challenges us to courageously go beyond the known into the mystery of wisdom, the immeasurable quality of life. It is a sacred power, the unconditional positive energy of the universe, the catalyst of existence and the longing of the ecological web of life. For me, love and spirit emanate from the same force—an abstract unifying power in nature. Love calls us to serenity and harmony, essential for health.

As love is freely flowing in the total ecosystem, we need to take the responsibility to be willing and active participants in this cycle of positive energy. Love will lead the way, gently and persistently offering opportunities to change and grow. I, as an adult, have a choice whether I answer the call. Often, that takes courage, as I confront my behavior and my beliefs, sometimes even my selfishness. Taking that courage in both hands, honestly contemplating my way of being in the world and committing myself to emerging into a healthier way of being is loving myself as an equal.

We cannot change many factors in our environment, or indeed our history, but the love energy demands we have responsibility to change what we can in and around ourselves. This energy is both practical and creative and can offer healing and deep reflection. I often use creative expression as a means of achieving understanding. The insight I have received from my grandfather's shoulders has only been possible because of unconditional love.

When authentic love is understood, compassion is possible. To give or be touched by compassion, someone who is willing to walk with you, to invest their whole self in you, is a deeply ecological and powerful experience. It is greater than sympathy, greater than empathy. It is the quality of suffering with another in the presence of love so that love's energy can heal. In both my personal and professional life, I have offered my compassionate self to others. The result is not in my hands, and indeed, all my energy goes into the offering. Much depends on how the other receives that compassion. At times, all love can do is hold the space, brim full of opportunity.

A whisper of love, a kindly thought.
A compassionate act, the miracle unsought.

We are all miracles when I think about it. Our human bodies are intricate and magnificent. Then there is the delightful part of us which can never be measured. We all have endless potential beyond our earthly understanding. We tend to limit ourselves at times because of old dynamics or fear of rejection. Unless we suspend learned habitual thoughts and genetic and generational patterns, change will not be possible, for we remain chained to the lineal dimension of the genomic paradigm. We will arrive at the place we came from, caught in our own web.

We need a place where our soul can find peace. We can achieve this within ourselves, yet we long to share this with another. This is intimacy, our physical, emotional and spiritual capacity to love and be loved. Intimacy is not a destination, a possession or a status. It is a direction, a learning. I recognise humbly that my life has been blessed by many people of all ages with whom I have walked the path of intimacy and they with me.

My grandfather once told me that age is not a number, it is a state of mind. He believed we are as young as our hope and as old as our fear, as young as our faith and as old as our uncertainties, as young as our knowledge and as old as our wisdom. He spoke from experience. As a four-year-old child, he had been left in a boarding school in New Zealand while his parents went to England. If he had remained in that place of abandonment, he would never have had the vision of the gift he gave me at the beach so long ago. He had reclaimed his spirit.

When our spirit is awake, we experience an inner all-inclusive consciousness, a powerful connection with the timeless center of the ever-present web of existential changing facets in our daily life. That touch allows the spirit of the present to offer the wholeness of wisdom in a rhythmic harmony of freedom to be in the moment with all of life. Wisdom offers the breath of life, deep knowing, being fully aware, feeling valuable and connected to the pure energy of love, the creative power of the universe. That creativity enables transcendence over the effects of history, forming a new oneness of the self. The key to this process is the recovery of spontaneity. When that door opens, our expression of the transcendent reflects harmony and presence. We practice being in the light, the great unfolding where we can see clearly.

We are all bearers of light. Yet, we will all have that light challenged by the shadows. I have experienced my share of the latter and I have learned that the more I choose to live in the light of truth, integrity, justice and transparency, the more I am challenged. I note the shadows, but they never have my full attention, for they can be mesmeric, even enticing. I will take my light to the edge, channel it into the shadows, but I never cross the line.

Twenty years ago, I was awakened out of an alarming shadow challenge by one of my granddaughters. We were on a ferry on the Noosa River when I pointed out a houseboat I particularly liked. She immediately said, "Nan, it's for sale!" My reply was, "Oh, I didn't want to own it."

She responded very quickly, looking me straight in the eye, "Why not, Nan?" Subsequently, she wrote down the number, handed it to my husband and said, "Pops, you need to buy this for Nan!" Twenty years later, we are frequently on the houseboat, a simple existence, close to the rhythm of the tides and to the natural world. Each sunrise brings new life, new beauty and new awareness. It is a gift of love and healing, reclaiming the light, brought through one child to another who stands on her grandfather's shoulders. Ubuntu indeed!

Whispers of love, our longing awake,
And streams of living water make.

Those streams have inexhaustible power, and when used with compassion, offer many opportunities. My grandfather was mindful of and discussed social issues but also taught me that to reach my higher self was both compassionate to the world and responsible to the spirit. He encouraged me to quietly reflect on my words, often spoken in youthful enthusiasm. I realise now he was introducing me to the passage into wisdom.

Our individual crescendos relate to the micro scale from where observations, emotions, thoughts, ideas and spiritual beliefs emerge, interrelate and transform. Employing that quiet reflection enables me to respond, rather than react. Reactions are often primal and not filtered through the value system. Universal dynamics manifest at the macro scale of existence, yet everything we do, say and enact affects the environment.

Mindfulness through concentration keeps us focused and opens the peerless value of soulful contemplation. Meditation and prayer in the quietness and sacredness of the self attracts what we need for the journey—inspiration which challenges intention. This was clearly indicated in my present path to healing. Love helps us make choices for the greater good and for ourselves.

Through this higher function comes inspiration. Inspiration is a circular energy, not centered in a physical place and not subject to cause and effect. It seems to come out of nowhere! It contains the seed of wisdom, of which Wendy is aware. It stimulates creativity, stirring new attractors to consider and the vortex continues if there is intention for wisdom. But this wisdom requires awareness in our inner experiential sacred space.

I honor with deep appreciation all the people who have offered their shoulders on which to stand. We are a company of people who offer simplicity in the turmoil, love in the confusion and light in the darkness. Undoubtedly, my grandfather, in his invitation to swim with him all those years ago, offered me the greatest gift of all:

"Wendy, fight the waves and you might drown. Go with them and they'll take you where you need to be."

Margaret Williams

Margaret Wendy Williams lives a "swinging" life between a house-boat on the Noosa River and a bush block near Bauple, a small rural town an hour and a half north. She was born in Queensland. Her passions include gardening, reading, music and being with people.

She initially trained as a teacher in Queensland and has taught at every level from preschool to tertiary education. Her passion was special education and she traveled to Prince George in Canada to teach for a year to save enough money to undertake further training in England. It took her twenty-five years to get to England, as she met her husband, John. They have been married for fifty-five years and delight in their family of two children, six grandchildren and one great-grandchild.

Upon leaving school, she wanted to be a social worker. When her children had grown up, she undertook that study, did further training in counseling and worked in that field for twenty-five years. She developed a unique program to assist survivors of child abuse to reclaim themselves from their abruptly interrupted lives, based on creative expression.

She has lived in four states and territories in Australia, Canada and Oregon, USA, always investing herself in community.

Upon retirement, encouraged by a friend, she enrolled in a Master of Arts (Social Ecology). This magnificent experience enabled her to weave her life tapestry into a whole.

At her final residential school in her study, she had the privilege of learning from Professor Martin Prozesky, who chose ubuntu as his topic. She delights in being part of this unique ubuntu publication.

THE TRUTH ABOUT TRUTH

JEN HAGEN

Pouring my cereal on a Saruday morning, the smell of sweet hot coffee wafted over my palate as she lowered the mug from her mouth. The collar of her burgundy terrycloth robe wrapped as high around her perfectly olive-toned neck as possible.

"Have any good dreams?" she asked as I poured my 2%. Most mornings were pretty quiet and conversation was scarce, unless there was a dream involved. It was a cloudy Pacific Northwest morning but the sun was peeking through and her rheumatoid symptoms and migraines seemed to be playing nice, so I bit.

"Yeah. A weird one. You?"

"Oh, you know, just the typical George stuff. Out on the prairie, living in a teepee with my ancestors." Her daydreamy face looked so content. "My dad was there too, but off in the distance."

At that time her dad had been gone for over seven years, and I could tell it seemed like eighty to her. She was raised by him and his mother on indigenous sacred prairies here in Washington state. Her Cowlitz lineage was a point of pride for her and so was her relationship with her dad. "He taught me everything I know ... a great man," she would say. "He always trusted me."

She often retold the story of her teen self and some girlfriends climbing up the capitol stairs to the top of the dome. They got out their lipstick and started writing on the marble walls and were caught. She told her dad the truth, that she didn't write on the walls with them, and he believed her. This was something she felt moved to share with us anytime she sensed we were being less than honest. My five siblings and I were raised to be honest and to earn trust, but on the flip side of that coin was a unique interpretation of the word truth and a suspicious philosophy about when and where telling the truth was appropriate. I was never taught how to decipher this and it got me into a lot of trouble.

Grandpa Byrd passed of a heart attack while hiking on Mount Saint Helens when I was only ten. Yes, that's the mountain that blew her top in 1980, only a few years later. From our house, the plume of volcanic ash looked like the pictures of Hiroshima I had seen in school. We were at least one hundred miles away and had over an inch of ash fall on our deck by the end of the day.

He loved the pristine Spirit Lake that I hiked with my kids thirty years later. It resembled more of a muddy stump and tree graveyard than the crystal-clear glacier water surrounded by old growth evergreens he frequented before the eruption.

Like the volcano, one blast wiped out her life force, and her gaze resembled the tree graveyard after he died. His spirit was still crystal clear in her dreams, and being in a teepee on the prairie with the love of her life and her father in the background must've felt like heaven on earth.

She only granted herself permission to live the dream while sleeping. Real life was for being responsible. True love, true freedom and a true pain-free life were extravagances she never afforded herself, so naturally truth had a sting she kept under tight reins.

My favorite trick growing up was to ask people how old they thought she was. She was incredibly gorgeous, and most people guessed incorrectly to which I loudly blurted out her true age which fell ten to fifteen years later than their guess. She hated birthdays and the reminders that she was getting older. In fact, I planned a surprise fortieth birthday party for her. Friends and family waited at the house for over three hours and she didn't show up. When I finally got ahold of her she told me, "I didn't want a birthday party." And I learned exactly what NOT to do: surprise her. I knew better than to spring things on her or ask her permission in front of other people, she remained calmly collected in her consistent response … NO. Surprises were a no-no. So, naturally a surprise party was too much and so was a nine-year-old telling all the attendees that the guest of honor, her mom, wasn't coming.

Emotions and privacy were kept under lock and key and I was typically scolded for trying to pick the lock to find my own truth by accessing hers. "Oh, I blocked that out," was often her response to my queries.

That or, "Why do you ask so many questions?"

So I loved these mornings; just her and me and our dreams at the table. I felt like we could talk about anything as long as it was in a dream.

Too bad I didn't figure that out earlier because I might have made a lot of shit up just to see what she thought of it. But I wasn't a good liar— one way I was more like her than my real mom.

Her breakfast fancied an over easy egg with buttered toast to dip in the runny yolk which was covered in salt. Lots of salt. The ionic bane of my existence. Like her father who passed of a heart attack suddenly at age sixty-five, she had extremely high blood pressure. A symptom of her diet and her clogged emotional pathways. I spent most of my years growing up trying to nutritionally police her diet, and as she grew less capable of navigating her medical schedule, I was the sibling who gladly volunteered for the job. My potent pursuit of keeping her alive was a perfect segue for my pursuit of a medical degree. I figured if she was my most difficult patient, I could handle anything. And she was definitely that.

Terrified of doctors, she seemed even more afraid of their probing questions and once the physician entered the exam room, the truth conveniently exited. She would flat-out lie to the doctors, telling them she was "fine", had "no pain" and that she "just wanted to get dressed and go home now". If I shook my head with eyes wide open, so they got the message that I strongly disagreed, she would whip her head around and stare me down like she was going to spank my adult ass right there for disobeying her cardinal rule: if you're not asked for the truth then BE QUIET.

As my mom's memory faded, so did her deep emotional wounds and the ability to hold resentment. Like a thick fog on a Pacific Northwest morning, the cloud of her potent experiences lifted and left a hole where the unfiltered light of her presence was allowed to shine again; she giggled more and told stories freely. One day when I was visiting, she blurted out with a smile, "Did I ever tell you about the worst day of my life?"

Equally surprised and curious, I responded with, "No … you didn't."

The story poured out of her in the most auspicious way; a story I'd waited my whole life to hear. In my fifty years I'd heard many unconnected details from different family members. I wondered if withholding details was her way of protecting me, but now I know she was protecting her five-year-old self, who saw the truth of deep emotions as dangerous, and every bone in her body held onto that belief. Any unwelcomed expression was swiftly dealt with as to keep our family, and her business, under the radar. Even at the end of her life, with her sodium levels dangerously low from an infection, I was scolded by my siblings for calling 911 and hence, alerting the neighbors of her business. We were all clear on the rules, but as the revolutionary, I felt saving her life warranted breaking them.

At age twenty-three, she was already the mom of five kids, a scout leader of four boys, a wife, daughter, daughter-in-law, friend, neighbor and owner of two adult purebred rough collies which we later showed and bred. Chaos was never something she allowed, even in the midst of "doing it all" but the sister role was a stressor that put the icing on the top of her fallen maternal cake.

Being the firstborn of my mom's half-sister and then raised as her youngest was confusing enough without the dividend visits my real mother inflicted upon us. I called her my aunt, and she always brought with her my "half-brother cousin"—a nickname she made up to try and clarify the family tree—quite unsuccessfully, I might add. She would drop information bombs like, *they made me give you up,* or, *I named you Jennifer, not Jenny,* to etch in my mind where I came from. This territorial claim on me never put me at ease or helped me feel like I belonged.

It was a lot for little me to dismantle. I saw myself as the youngest of six not a drop-in daughter of her aunt … but I was both and no one was allowed to forget it. Most of my friends had a very simple, straightforward story of belonging. I wanted that.

My belonging was clearly under negotiation, depending upon who you spoke to in my family.

My real mom was my grandma's favorite, so naturally so was I. I was always happy to see her come pick me up to take me to her beach house with my grandpa. I was also always pleasantly surprised when my real mom would show up to visit, but wondered why my older siblings did not come with us.

My mom was the epitome of the word mom and integrity, but the little girl she resembled as the long-awaited story of my life came pouring out of her that day helped me see why trust was something she clung to. And why, like many, she was determined to do a complete 180 from her own mother's path.

To say something was "the worst day of her life" was a pretty big deal.

I had only heard it said one time before and that was when she accompanied me to help my five-year-old daughter go under anaesthesia for the first time.

A hospital setting for dental work was the only option then because, at the time, her inability to speak left her prone to fits of fight, flight and freeze all at once, when her tender sensory system was triggered. My mom had a big soft spot for my kids and would have done anything for them, but that day was obviously a stretch which sent her blood pressure sky-high.

Although she navigated A LOT, there were certain things that were just "too much"—difficult emotions, social injustice and medical procedures. She said she "never wanted to do that again", after we left the hospital and I didn't blame her … four hours of nurses trying to convince me that everything was going to be "fine, easy and safe" while trying to convince my highly alert daughter to simply drink a "little grape sedation cocktail". I had informed the pre-op team several times of the unlikelihood of her cooperation. There were beds, curtains, screams, holds and several staff trying to force liquid down my little girl's throat while she struggled her way free and ran away over and over. I think every little girl in the place was triggered.

I remember my mom having sensory issues of her own. She threatened to pop our balloons if we didn't keep them quiet in the car because she hated the sound of our skin against them. The smell of thrift stores made her indignantly nauseous because as she put it, "Gaaahd! It smells like everyone's house in here."

Our house never had a smell, she made sure of that! Pledge and Pine-Sol accompanied the perfectly blended voices that spun from within our dark walnut console stereo. The outside shined as much as the stars that graced her album covers; Mama Cass was her favorite. I loved her taste in music—clean with a hint of lemon-scented California Dreamin'.

Music was one of the few places where deep emotions were allowed to be expressed at our house, so naturally we were all drawn to it.

Our voices were required to blend into her perfectly kept home, but she was more of a hyper-intuitive dictator than a reactive one. She could sense an emotional storm brewing in any of us and shoot a single "hey!" into the air and we would all freeze knowing that whatever we were doing wrong was on her radar, but making a scene was not her style. Her extra-sensory momming comforted me, and despite her critical analysis of my overshares, I saw myself in that intuitive part of her. I was always trying to find parts of her that fit me.

Like the shifting faults under the mountain that unleashed a steamy blast strong enough to flatten ten thousand feet of old growth forest—the implosive story of her sister's fault swept fifty years of burning questions into a sea of deep dirt I didn't see coming.

"Well, you know how she used to drop you off and say, 'can you take Jenny for a few days?' ... that's how it always went. A few days turned into a few weeks ... then months and well ... years for you," she giggled then looked me straight in the face and said, "Well, you have another brother."

"I know, Mom," I interrupted, thinking this was just a little memory lapse moment for her. "I knew him ... remember? He was born when I was five ... my ... 'brother cousin!?'" I said with added air quotations so she would laugh.

"NO NO NO. Not him. There's another one in-between you two."

"WHAT?!"

"Yes. She brought him home to me too, just like she did with you. The usual few days became a few weeks, and I loved that baby so much, just like I did each one of you, but we just couldn't keep another baby ... we could barely afford the six of you."

The pace of her speech slowed way down and I felt a tide of sludgy shame wash in.

"When he was six months old she showed up out of the blue and said she was going to give up the baby. I loaded up what I could of the baby's and we just got in the car and drove to a parking lot. The Lutheran adoption van pulled up and a man got out and gave her some papers to sign. As soon as she was done, he took the baby from my arms, got in the van and drove away. It was horrible. I could barely believe it was happening

... but it happened."

"Mom! How? That would be so hard. And how could she do that ... again?"

"I don't know, I've never been able to understand her but I knew she could do the same thing to you and that scared me to DEATH. I'll never get over how I felt when he took that baby and drove away. We had to go to court to adopt you because I was not going to let her do that to you."

And there it was, the mother wound of all mother wounds. The fear that I would be taken from her. The pain in her eyes when I reminded her of her sister, which reminded her I was not hers. My grandma picking only me up to go to the beach.

I thought of all those times people told me I looked like my mom and I responded with, "I look even more like my real mom." A truth we all knew but I said out loud, perhaps to recallibrate and come to terms with the maternal chaos my life represented.

At the end of my mom's life and not too long after she shared about that day, we were sitting at the foot of her bed going through the contents of a chest. It was filled with old photos and memorabilia, but that day she opened it up and handed me a manila envelope with *Jenny and the kids* written in her perfect cursive.

She had thoughtfully sifted through all her pictures, cards and letters dated back to her grandparents and compiled an envelope full of generational gems for each of her six kids.

I sifted through it with her. There were photos of my kids, my real mom, me as a baby, at Halloween, at the beach, in Girl Scouts and several other family gems. There were letters I wrote to her in college, pieces of construction paper with Mother's Day poems written in crayon and some printed from a computer ... Mother's Day poems from the time I was in kindergarten until my own kids were in kindergarten.

She kept every single one.

My elementary school report cards were filed in order with the common comments: *Could do better work,* and, *Talks too much.*

My third-grade teacher, however, who is still my favorite, had a hand-written note saying, *Jenny is lovely but seems quieter lately. Could something at home be bothering her?*

That was the year my parents divorced, and I wasn't able to see my dad for over a year because of his alcoholism. Insightful of her to offer me the benefit of the doubt, rather than checking the boxes I already had etched into my psyche:

✓ Too much of a tomboy.

✓ Too much expression of my feelings.

✓ Too nosy.

✓ Too hyper.

✓ Too much like my real mom.

I pulled out a few black-and-whites of my grandma as a tween and another of her in her early twenties. What a stunner. A combination of Doris Day and Lucille Ball: lipstick, red hair, costume jewelry, true movie-star style. It was rumored that before I was born, she had seven husbands. No surprise looking at these photos, or by the way she laughed loud and played cards till all hours with friends at the beach. The sisters shared her looks but it was often stated aloud that my real mom was more fun than her older sister. Fun was another family concept that had conflicting interpretations.

The span of my poems reiterated my adoration for her, stating how pretty, young and beautiful she was … and of course, kind. That was a given. I owed her my life and I knew it at a very young age.

I opened a portrait of my mom in a cardboard frame that still smelled like my grandparents' house—pipe tobacco and beach grass. Written inside was, *To Mother, Love Barbara.* I thought to myself, *Mother?! Geez, how formal!*

I had never used that word, not even Mommy or Mama. My mom had always been Mom because my teenage siblings called her that.

"Hey, Mom? What did you think of grandma when you were young?" I asked as I stared at her pre-marriage, pre-mom, pre-worst-day-of-her-life, trusted daughter's face that had spunk … innocence. Her big brown eyes looked up and her head tilted to access the memory of who she was in the picture.

A sweet smile swept across her face, "Oh," she sighed, "I thought she was SO BEAUTIFUL and I just wanted her to love me."

Wow. I expected her typical short, evasive response, but the memory-loss mom was able to remember feelings AND remain open to inquiry, which was both refreshing and sad because I knew she was letting go of this life. Typically, when I expressed hopeful ideas she'd come with, "You didn't get that liberal thinking from me," but I HAD. I was one hundred percent HERS: a tender, tenacious lover of truth, music, mountains, and dreams, just like she was … and a great mom. Responsibility was a heavy baton she handed me along with a reliance upon coffee and humor to manage the pain, and I grasped it as a token of belonging. But at the core I wanted MORE. She and I both did. Our common ground was that each of us had a sweet, smitten, little girl in us, who just wanted her mother to love her. Mine did. And that's the truth.

Jen Hagen

J en has had a vlog, a podcast, a website and many online branches where she openly shared about her life and the life of her family as they barreled through adventure after adventure from school to medicine to outdoor adventures she has risked to gain in her hero's journey.

In fact, Joseph Campbell inspired her life mantra, "Say yes to it all."

Jen's most recent dream was inspired by one question her dear friend and inspiration asked her, "Jen what breaks your heart?" Tererai Trent unravelled a deep wound with that question and as Jen wrote the answer, the question went deeper and deeper, until she buried it in the ground like Tererai. By seeing her in the ubuntu way, asking her that potent question and then being present with her answer, Tererai helped her birth her truth and say yes to the embodiment of her broken heart's fire where all the solutions lie.

Since she was small, Jen has followed the paths of the great social justice leaders, revolutionaries and poets in the world, but none were as influential as her own two children in facilitating her awakening.

Their true hearts reflected back to her everything important, led her to transformational people, invigorating experiences and gave her a sacred focus in life.

Her biggest vision has yet to physically manifest and is called DragonFLY landing. It is an outdoor adventure custom neighborhood for families like hers and is based in the principles of presence she learned and is still learning from saying Yes to it all.

Poetry is the way Jen puts her expansive visions into words, so here are a few streams of loving kindness with ubuntu energy running through them.

Please accept this gift, and share with a mama in your life. We all stand on the shoulders of many many mamas who had the courage to say yes … to themselves, and to us.

namaste

the mother in me
recognizes the mother in you
the breathing
bleeding
leading-edge madre
Dante's heat has nothing on you
brewing solutions in the palm of your right hand
while tenderly touching the cheek of every child with your left
tiny faces in love with yours
you never fail to effortlessly release a smile from that fragile frame of a fortress
a portal for prayers
a pinnacle with layers that embrace faults and fright
only to embody their field of vision
and make it your mission to love more
i adore your vigor

Ubuntu

a trigger can never keep you down
essence
meets lessons
and bows to blessed life
the kind you carry
buried within you are seeds of change
maintain your flow
dream to know that
you mama
are the line to all things that glow
in your eternal gaze is a blaze no twist of fate could furl
so take your twirl under the stars
far and wide is your reach
blow dandelion seeds
to barefoot dreams spilt on every grain of sensual sand you crash into
trust the wind to move malignant mountains
while you
the maverick
dance in your fountain
of eternal truth
      ~zj (jen hagen) on Mother's Day ~ 5:55 am to 6:27 am ~ 2022

a song

of silver foxes
serving chicken soup
to the souls of their offspring
DNA to RNA to DNA again
the beat goes on
harmonious as the hummers' whispery chirps
we slurp up nurtured pines

our shrines rich with insense and nonsensical omens
shamans dance on graves
as she takes in the gazes of her clan
her span is far and wide
open
eternal dawn paints shadows in the sky
as her why buys time on luminary leaves of absinthe
a score straight from heaven's pelvic floor
orchestrated with stars and seeds
her deeds are stunning
she bleeds a running brook
into hereditary alphabet stew
thick with worry and woo woo

moi
plus vous
equals us

the family truss

Majestic
Altruistic
Medicinal
Alchemist

MAMA
an intrepid brew

8/3/23 12:19 AM ~ me

OPPORTUNITY TO RISE UP

RAQUELLE ROULETTE

C ollege wasn't an option for people like me. Though I knew other students were making those next-step plans through the past few weeks and months, my attention was on more pressing issues. *Just one day, one step at a time,* I told myself. My full name rang out—loud—over the intercom, piercing silence and concentration.

She brought the corded phone up to her ear, and for a minute or two, muffled words were exchanged that I couldn't make out. It was a clear effort to be discreet, not just consideration for volume—which raised more concern. My heart sank, skipping a beat, when she said I should go now without finishing my test.

After shuffling to quickly pack up and bringing the incomplete assignment to her desk, my bulky backpack was hauled over one shoulder. Carrying my belongings with me, as I always did, was a habit of necessity; best to keep my things close in case I wouldn't be returning. Its cumbersome weight was the least of my worries. Something told me whatever reason I was unexpectedly being called out of class and into the guidance and advising counselors' office would take a while.

Requirements for graduation couldn't be what this was about. At our most recent appointment, I was reassured that I was on track to earn my diploma. I also learned I would rank within my graduating class' top 2%.

We had yet to talk about college preparation, plans for summer, or any leisure topics, though; two months from now, or past graduation, was too far into the future for me to give attention to. And even still, none of that would be time-sensitive enough to interrupt a test.

With everything going on—some things the school counselors were and were not aware of—I knew this wasn't likely to be good. The last time something similar happened, child protection caseworkers had just left my siblings' school, taking my brother and sister's statements before pulling me out of class to collect and corroborate the same information from me. I stood briefly in the hallway, taking a few slow breaths to steady my heart rate, and considered potential causes for the sudden interruption. Heavy thumping and out-of-rhythm beating meant I'd soon be light-headed if the tachycardia episode didn't pass.

Wondering what could be more important than finishing one of my last exams, I couldn't avoid thinking about that last time. I was requested to go to the office before being questioned about my parents, situations involving family, home circumstances, and childhood experiences occurring behind closed doors. They wanted to know about our home lives, if our needs were met, and if we were being cared for appropriately. We had been through this before.

That most recent time wasn't the first time, either, and nothing helpful had ever resulted from the transparency. Somebody made a report about possible abuse, so they found me at school, asked hours of questions, filled notepads with details, then talked with our parents—sharing many of those details with them—and left us to deal with the aftermath. My stomach turned from the anxiety triggered just by hearing my name come through the intercom.

If protective services were back for a report, it was always hard to know what, or how much, to say. And we didn't want our mom in trouble. Or anyone, for that matter. Our lifestyle resulted from the best they knew how to do, with the knowledge and resources they had accessible.

We wanted help and were always truthful, but we also needed peace inside the home.

The situation, everywhere I turned, was so delicate. What would justice or sincere help look like, anyway? Maybe I'd be sent away, handed over to someone else to endure a different kind of trauma. Or, likely, we'd all be separated. Outside of our parents' household and unrelated to any inquiries involving them, despite sharing truths and hoping to protect my siblings, I had to live knowing my grandfather was still enjoying the rest of his life freely.

Many relatives who had previously cared for me didn't know what to believe about the allegations. They probably didn't want to think about it or risk getting involved, and I couldn't fault them for keeping their peace. I didn't know what *pedophilia* meant at twelve years old, but I knew what had been happening on and off for years. Four was too young to know it wasn't normal, and age fourteen was the last time I saw anyone from that half of the family.

I wondered if the police didn't pursue initial statements due to my grandfather's income for good legal defense, my grandmother's description of me—"the lying homewrecker"—once she heard, or because I was swiftly sent out of state to a different family member before they could carry out a real investigation. Two years after the first report, my mom and stepfather, with my siblings, had nowhere else to go but back to that city. My grandparents could help them gain stability. An aunt in the area fought and succeeded in taking me in, showing me support and decency. My family, with my brother and sister, were sharing a home with a now-outed alleged sexual offender.

A month into freshman year there, after an emotional confrontation led by my grandmother, I confided in a woman at school—a counselor and mandated reporter—and the investigation opened again. Within a few days, I was shipped onto another plane by myself, facing many unknowns. Ultimately, speaking up about the situation complicated the balance, elevating risks for everyone. It wasn't a matter of right or wrong; I tried to understand. I didn't know then that I would attend four schools that ninth-grade year. The system sometimes fails children like us.

Walking to the office, trying to settle my nerves, I sorted possibilities in my mind. With straight-A grade reports going back as far as I could remember, this trip to the counseling department must be unrelated to academics. Other students talked about college, but I knew they met with guidance counselors and their parents to arrange those plans.

No one in my family went to college or earned any degree. I *had* been told education, in general, was the way out toward a different lifestyle. Still, I was clueless about how to pay for it or any of that. And where would I live? Despite a strong affinity for learning, I never considered further schooling feasible. It was ruled out, not taken seriously as a possibility; I hadn't seen anyone make it happen.

People like me had to go straight to work. Life is a matter of day-to-day survival for so many, and I didn't question limiting beliefs. All anyone can be expected to know is what they are exposed to. I knew if I couldn't depend on family or anyone else, I could rely on myself and at least find a way to make enough money to get by. I was curious if counselors wanted to discuss the idea of college. I honestly hadn't considered it.

With no one to hold me accountable, I stayed out of trouble to avoid liability and self-sabotage. That most recent report was initiated from my siblings' school, and we were each questioned. After my parents were approached, though, the fault fell on me as the oldest and most transparent. The caseworker documented that my mom and stepfather *wanted me removed from their home.* I saw the paperwork. I was an *out-of-control teenager.* Everything was all turned around and backward.

It was written that things I said weren't credible. They *didn't want me to be their responsibility,* and I *was the cause of our chaos.* After years of standing up to my stepdad—for myself, my mom and my siblings—against physical and verbal abuse, I was labelled *disrespectful and defiant* in the notes. Someone had described me as *a drug-addicted prostitute who would sell myself for a Big Mac*. And I had *a history of making up false allegations*, referencing the unresolved situation involving my grandfather a few years previous. It was assumed, too, that cardiac symptoms were made-up or exaggerated. I remembered the handwriting in the margins and their signatures as I walked toward the school's second floor, preparing myself for who knows what.

My parents' version, painting me as a negative example and source of our issues, cost me six months of returning "home" once a day to be present for "therapeutic family services". The program's mission was to improve the lives of troubled youth through residential, family-focused services. Our problems were generational and deep. Through mandated and short-lived group therapy, attempting to shed any light on the real issues only worsened conditions in private family life.

I had peace when the juvenile officer found me at a location I was staying temporarily and requested the drug screening without forewarning. He brought me directly to the facility, where I passed the drug test with flying colors. I didn't get an apology, but I didn't have to return to their care, either. Essentially on my own at sixteen, I wasn't sure where I would sleep most days, but I stayed focused on school and kept moving forward.

Enlistment in the military, as my father had done, seemed like the best, most possible theory for my life if I could make it to the end of summer when my shipment date for boot camp was tentatively scheduled. I didn't know what else to do. The military would provide a living, a place to live, and maybe college tuition one day.

Last month, I completed recruitment paperwork, despite symptoms of what I believed was a serious heart condition. When I managed to find rides to specialist appointments an hour away, doctors' assessments, without the ability to see evidence of the random and periodic episodes, couldn't provide any diagnosis. So, I was cleared medically, satisfied the physical requirements, took all the tests, and passed final background checks.

I swore into the United States Navy with a 93 ASVAB score and the highest security clearance. I just had to wait for high school graduation to leave. I had no clue what else this unanticipated meeting could be about, but it felt significant. I hoped it wouldn't jeopardize enlistment or cause me to leave the area before graduation. This school was already my twenty-third.

Approaching the top of the stairs, nearing whatever I was about to face in the office, I grounded myself by focusing only on what I could control: my mindset and perspective. I counted my blessings, naming them one by one. My personal life lacked routine, and things didn't always work out how I wanted, but I couldn't think of a time I didn't have what I needed. As I felt appreciation and gratitude for each idea on my list, my heart rate began to steady, fortunately falling back into a normal rhythm. I took another slow breath, savoring the calm before opening the door to the office.

I closed the door behind me and was greeted by three women with warm smiles. I was expecting a different energy in the room. The two counselors kindly and gently asked me to have a seat. Confused, I sat across from the third woman, who looked vaguely familiar.

They explained that Ms. Rebecca, a mutual friend's mom, was there to ask if I would stay with her until graduation or until I left for the military. She heard from her son that I didn't have a place to live. Empathizing with me in my situation, she was there to help. A woman I had met only once showed up, offering a safe, stable space with her inside their home.

The next few months were a blur. On graduation day, dressed in my red cap and gown, I thought about how these moments were a product of so many individuals pouring into my life. Each colorful cord draped across my shoulders, and any of the accomplishments they represented, symbolized encouragement and motivation from others. We are at our best when we can rely on the wisdom, knowledge, and understanding of those around us. I still couldn't believe I was receiving my high school diploma in a few minutes.

Making it this far had been unimaginable because young women in my family hadn't yet had these experiences. And we can't see what we don't know. It was inside the houses of many who shared with me that I found home, development, and life's most essential lessons. I fully acknowledged my good fortune and the significance—because we are, I am. The opportunity to hear my name read was one step forward, and it was hope. I walked across the stage.

***

The incredible news brought me to tears. My oldest child, three and a half years old, sat quietly in the chair beside me; the baby was in her car seat carrier at my feet. Twenty-five years young with two small children and in the middle of a domestically abusive relationship, we were backed into a corner.

With no real job since my daughter's birth and "only" my high school diploma, we would be headed to the women's shelter if I couldn't make something happen for us and fast. The situation at home squeezed all but the life out of me. He didn't even know we were at the college today, but it was time for me to evaluate every possible solution. I had been told a fake name and age, verified by a forged ID, and believed the information for a whole year until learning the truth after our daughter was conceived. I shouldn't have been so naive—stuck in a bad relationship founded on dishonesty, the stress and uncertainty I felt now resulted from irresponsible choices and impatience to find real love.

Caring for the children alone left me constrained on time. Juggling odd jobs and donating plasma on a schedule limited our finances. Waiting for him to pay bills when he wouldn't keep a job or prioritize the home left us vulnerable. Now finally, without our own vehicle, I needed to do anything to take steps to get out of this situation.

Asking questions and researching within the community for resources uncovered a few decent options. I considered a CNA class or a short phlebotomy certification; I could draw blood at the plasma center instead of donating. I knew I could work in fast food or waitress at a restaurant. For child care, I could secure a spot in a local income-based day care. The last good option was applying for a scholarship.

The flier posted at the Department of Workforce Services said, *Adult Education Entrepreneurship Scholarship.* I didn't think it involved real school or a college—the scholarship was intended to cover courses for a twelve-month online certificate program. "Entrepreneurship," I had no idea what that was, but *adult education ...* I thought; *Hey, I'm an adult trying to be educated.* I felt qualified enough to apply for whatever education they offered, and an online certificate seemed manageable. I couldn't change my entire situation right now or make a big commitment, but this would be a step toward growth.

I scrambled to put my application together nicely before the deadline, turning in the complete application on the last hour of the final day, not realizing adult education students are people who don't yet have their GED. I was honest in my application and essay, including that I graduated high school. I detailed the circumstances since earning my diploma, including medical procedures and recovery related to a rare heart condition and then losing my first child's father to suicide during the pregnancy. I did my best to communicate the sincere need and desire for the education they could provide.

After the award letter arrived, Jeff, a gentleman I met waitressing, graciously loaned me a vehicle. I headed to Pulaski Technical College, two kids in tow, to sign up for the certificate courses. Walking into the building, hearing a lecture down the hall, I thought, *How exciting—It feels like school here! It even smells like school.* Smiling, I was truly happy for the students, thinking about them and their learning in this space.

But I was just here for a short, online certificate program, not a true school experience or classes. *But that's okay. It's still progress,* I encouraged myself. I waited for an appointment with admissions and then the financial aid office. Talking with the aid counselor, and sitting there with my children, I'll never forget the overwhelming emotion that came next.

I found out I could apply those four free courses with other scholarships and aid … Toward a degree! I could go to college and get an actual college degree. I couldn't believe the news. I could even switch my online courses to be present in-person for class. I cried for ten minutes as I tried to comprehend what she was saying.

She told me people donated money for students like myself to help pay for classes and meet their needs while attending school. With my adult education scholarship and a government grant, tuition would be covered and I would receive a $2,400 refund for the first semester. And it was possible to earn more scholarships. Jeff would be happy to let me borrow his car while I started class on campus, and soon I'd have the money to get our own due to the generosity of donors and taking my education seriously.

I could also work part-time at the school and would always be welcome to volunteer with adult education students. It meant so much to be able to give back. I was in the last group of students to receive that particular scholarship.

The decision to fill out the application was trying one of the last options—anything—to gain independence and make ends meet for my children, a small effort hoping to change the trajectory of our family. Making unfamiliar choices was bringing my very best to the situation. Still, my best hadn't always seemed to be enough.

When it wasn't enough, others came through, lending support at the perfect times. Sir Isaac Newton said, "If I have seen further than others, it is because I have been standing on the shoulders of giants." Through the investment of others, now we had access to different information. It wouldn't be taken for granted.

Raquelle Roulette

R aquelle S H Roulette was born in Orange County, California, with the coolest last name—and began her fascination with reading and writing early. At age ten, she read all seven Harry Potter books within ten days. A student of life, she had also already witnessed her father's first suicide attempt, her mother's mental health diagnosis, was an accessory to drug smuggling across international lines, and attended four schools that fifth-grade year. She still credits reading to be a great escape, instrumental for education and leisure today.

Experiencing a variety of obstacles and challenges as a homeless youth, multiracial, first generation, and non-traditional, Raquelle faced a combination of adversity; nevertheless, she obtained a high school diploma as well as her first three college degrees, each with a perfect 4.0 grade average. She earned highest honors academically with no debt, a decade after high school, as a single parent to three children under five.

In addition to the pride and fulfillment of being Henry, Annie and Adonis' mom, and outside the home, believing community involvement to be essential, Raquelle finds her joy through mentorship and working closely with adult education students. As they earn a high school equivalency diploma and take foundational steps towards their goals, the investment rewards throughout the process. The privilege is witnessing the effects of simple empowerment and resulting self-reliance. Through meeting people where they are in their circumstance and giving support for the journey from an early stage, doors are opened to build financial literacy, career readiness skills and other tools enabling further wellness and personal successes.

An honors graduate of 2022, Raquelle earned three degrees from the University of Arkansas—Pulaski Technical College and is attending the University of Arkansas—Fayetteville on a full academic scholarship. Raquelle will earn a dual bachelor's degree from UARK Walton College of Business in 2024. Her interests are in business management, leadership, and non-profit.

Raquelle was nominated for fellowship on the Little Rock Mayor's College Council in 2022, and elected a North Little Rock chapter officer in Phi Theta Kappa international college honor society. The American Association of University Women (AAUW) selected Raquelle to represent her school with scholarship attendance to the National Conference for Women Student Leaders in 2021. Also in 2021, she was chosen as the annual recipient of UA-PTC's Academic All-Star Award, stacking the renewable transfer scholarship with a combination of others to fully fund her first four years of post-secondary education. This strategic planning and learning with intention earned Raquelle multiple university degrees, completely debt-free, with excess funding to supplement her in supporting her family of four as a full-time single parent and full-time honors student.

In 2023, she received an award at the Women Changing the World international recognition event held in London, United Kingdom, in the category of Social Enterprise. Her work as a speaker, writer, and advocate on the topics of education, wellness, and personal development go hand in hand with her efforts as a Baton Activator fundraising for Tererai Trent International. The non-profit organization provides essential scholarship funding for girls and those facing fewer opportunities, enabling them to earn a post-secondary education. Avidly pursuing her dreams, Raquelle became a published author in 2022 and 2023 with the release of *Sacred Promise*, *I am Queen*, and *Ubuntu* anthology books.

When she's not in class, working, maintaining her spiritual life or writing—in lieu of doing housework—Raquelle can be found cultivating more joy with her children, painting, ice-skating, gardening, or otherwise sowing seeds.

Raquelle's passion is within the mind and motivation of others to fight to grow themselves. Her work with Photographers for Humanity, an organization established in 2019 to document real life in its beauty and struggle, is to provide love and resources, viewing each life as piece of an expansive puzzle. We are stronger together, and we are one. Grateful for diversity and a variety of experiences, she believes we should do our part, however small, to share our strengths and lessons lived to help each other harness our full potential.

Website: thelovelyelle.com
LinkedIn: Raquelle Roulette
Instagram: @_lovely.elle
Facebook: Lovely Elle Roulette
Linktree: linktr.ee/raquelleroulette

INTERWOVEN

Shared Stories, Shared Humanity

KELLIE HACKNEY

As I close my eyes and think of ubuntu—I am because of who we are—I envisage a beautiful woven tapestry. A work in progress, a reflection of our journeys and a witness to the journeys we share together. As I look closer at the woven threads before me, each one interwoven with the next creating form and building story, capturing moments of meaning and bringing forth life. Each thread now a part of me and inseparable to the fabric of my life. Each thread uniquely its own, some silken and others coarse, others cocreated by strands being plaited together to create new threads. All representing an array of textures and colours reflecting the colours of the rainbow, some glistening and sparkling as they catch the light, yet others luminous with their own living light.

There was a time when the tapestry of my life was ripped and torn apart, threads hanging in every direction, a vision of disarray, confusion and knotted entanglement. Having experienced childhood trauma, my life had become an entanglement of pain and shame, and every day was a fight for survival. The survival strategies I was using were no longer working, my mental health was so poor that every day was a matter of life and death. My life was spiraling out of control with addiction, and I had disconnected from myself and was disconnecting from everyone around me.

I remember when the penny dropped, and I realised I was meant to be on the planet at this time and I stopped fighting against it. In that moment I had to dig deep and find my "why", the reason I'm alive and my purpose that which I sensed was far greater than myself. I took the frayed fibres of my life and began to weave, creating the masterpiece of my life with new threads of hope, possibility and wonder. What began was a journey of finding hope and believing in the possibility that my life could be different. I found hope, I look for and find it daily, and my life today is testament to possibilities. My purpose and that journey continues as I try to share the gift I've been given by planting seeds of hope and possibility for others. I'm so grateful for those who, during my darkest and stormiest days, reminded me of the sun coming up tomorrow and the rainbow that comes after the rain, days when I had forgotten what the sun looks like and my only desire was what was beyond the rainbow. At first, I didn't believe them and then I could only trust in the words as they continued to remind me and never gave up, I finally remembered the sun (and that it does so much more than cause sunburn) and I caught a glimpse of the rainbow.

Today, when dark times come, I look for stars while I wait for the sun to rise again, and I love when it rains because I get so excited to see a rainbow, and every now and then a friend will send me a rainbow or bring some sunshine along when the night has been long and the storm has set in. I was in my mid-twenties at the time, and now, having doubled those number of years, I see a beautiful tapestry forming before me, rich with treasures found in the darkness, guided by hope and possibility, and celebrating every day of life as the beautiful gift it is.

In celebrating the essence of ubuntu, I need to acknowledge some very special people who have crossed my path and the beautiful gifts they have given to not only me but to all humanity.

They are the illuminators, when their light shines it captures the imagination, their reflection and refraction sending out living light and color.

Illuminating and holding the space before you so you can create your own path forward. They remind me of the glowworms found in the darkest of places—during the day they are inconspicuous, but in the darkness these luminescent larvae sparkle, dotting caves, tunnels and walkways with blue-green light, a spectacular bioluminescence of living light.

They are the menders; they take the torn and broken and craft something so new it was better than what existed before. Imagine a child, heartbroken at having their favouite jeans destroyed after falling over and tearing them. When taken to the mender they are returned adorned with beautiful woven embellishments and the child is overwhelmed with getting back what they thought was destroyed but now the best thing they have ever seen.

They are the healers, the ones who've dedicated their lives to bringing and being a healing balm, a soothing ointment of care and compassion and whose presence brings remedy to the confusion, calamity and chaos of life.

They are igniters, creatives whose flame sparks fires everywhere and sets hearts on fire. These gifted individuals invite us on a journey, to explore, imagine and create what we had never dreamed possible.

The gift that each of the following people gave me is immeasurable and so valuable. They saw me, they looked beyond the symptoms, behaviors and damage and saw *me*. It wasn't about their role or the job they were doing, rather it was about who they are and who they invited me to be.

Marg—a living light and a kaleidoscope of colour who taught me how to see and be in the world.

I met Marg over twenty years ago when I was volunteering at a retreat in the Hunter Valley. Marg had come to work at the retreat as a counselor and over the following year had such a foundational impact on my life. I was in my mid-twenties at the time and I was a searching, trying to find purpose and trying to make meaning of my life. My life at the time mirrored the typical trajectory of someone who has experienced complex trauma. I was running and numbing and consumed by a suffocating cloak of shame. Marg interrupted that narrative and showed me a different way to see and be in the world. I remember when she shared with me a quote from Viktor Frankl's *Man's Search For Meaning*: "*Everything can be taken from a man or a woman but one thing; the last of human freedoms to choose one's attitude in any given set of circumstances, to choose one's own way.*" When I heard this, along with what I experienced in Marg's presence—unconditional love, compassion, a curiosity towards the mysteries of life and our spiritual journey and wonder at life's beauty—it awakened my moral imagination. It gave me hope and a way forward.

I recently caught up with Marg after twenty years and it was as though time had stood still. Immediately I was enveloped with a warm sensation of loving kindness, like I had been hugged from the inside out. A feeling beyond the realm of words but echoing her all familiar wisdom, compassion and loving kindness. Look out for Marg's chapter in this book, it is such an honor to write beside you, Marg.

Lorraine and David—God's love and the Christian message personified.

I met Lorraine and David just over twenty years ago when I moved to the Hunter Valley and was referred to their medical practice. I had recently come out of rehab and was trying to hold the shattered pieces of my life together and my mental health was spiraling out of control. Lorraine and David saw me at my lowest and in the darkest days of my life. Their compassion, care and love sheltered me until I could begin to show compassion, care and love to myself. They believed me, but more importantly, they believed *in* me. They didn't just see the unwell parts of me, they saw my gifts and skills and opened opportunities for me to experience contributing and giving back. This was pivotal to my healing journey. Several years ago, Lorraine and David started Kwila, a community-based rehab. A place where people in recovery from substance use disorder or at risk of relapse can come to connect, recover and contribute. It is an honor for me to volunteer and support this mission and vision. Twenty years later, I continue to witness Lorraine and David giving to others their beautiful gift of unconditional compassionate care and with the same amount of energy, fervor and dedication. I acknowledge and thank them both for bringing God's love and the Christian message to life and dedicating their lives in service to the most broken and outcast of our society.

Sharon—a way-maker, not around but through, together.

I met Sharon in a run-down old house on the grounds of the local hospital. She was a clinical psychologist who worked for the region's drug and alcohol service. Sharon was like a burst of sunshine, and her office was anything but clinical. It was filled with character, mystery and memories. Sharon didn't "treat" my disorder or work to fix the symptoms of my life. The gift she gave me was creating the space and safety to explore and adventure into what I called my madness. She helped me to unwrap, understand and celebrate my unique gifts including the creative and resourceful ways I had adopted and adapted to survive. It can be confronting to invite someone into your headspace and share with them your thinking, the weird (and she would say wonderful) ways that I constructed meaning and made sense of the injustice and challenges of life.

She taught me how to connect with myself to find and celebrate the parts of me that were so hidden I wasn't even sure I knew existed. Sharon helped me understand my body and mind's reaction to my lived experiences and to discover new ways of honoring these. She helped me to diss the "dis" in my life creating order from disorder and learning to function and carving my way through all the dysfunctions. In meeting me at places where there were no words, she sat with me in silence until I found my voice. The work was deep, and it was defining, but not through the labels of illness or experience, though. It was defining in the discovery and acceptance of my unique self and all that I bring to the world. I sense her delight and smile shining down from beyond the rainbow.

Felicity and Noula—the creatives the living lights and fire starters.

There is nothing more beautiful than seeing the glow and feeling the warmth of someone whose flame shines bright and is well alight. A flame which has been seeded in your heart. A flame ignited by your courage to dream and then dare to show the world. A flame seen and felt because of your generosity to share and give away. A flame of warmth and light which embodies your presence, energy in love. Yet … there is something more beautiful than your flame—the beacon of light's calming warmth and presence, starting fires everywhere. Without your knowledge or you even believing it possible. Your flame sparks and ignites a hope, a passion and a purpose to the flickering, smoldering and meandering flames you encounter. Fires begin spotting everywhere, but not with the fire from her own flame. Rather, a fire and flame that is authentically its own. Hearts coming alive, dreams being reimagined, women reclaiming themselves and their place. This! There's nothing more beautiful than this!

Glen—my partner in life, loudest cheerleader and friend and a special gift from God.

What was thought at first to be a moment of synchronicity, a meeting by chance, proved to be so much more; it was a connection orchestrated by the divine. Fifteen years ago I met the most incredible human, so strong yet so gentle, so normal yet so surprisingly and marvellously different. I wasn't looking for a relationship when I met Glen, but it was certainly meant to be. He was comfortable in his own skin and he invited me and showed me how to be comfortable in my own. He has brought stability, calm, love and laughter into my world and I'll be forever grateful for the opportunity to walk beside this special man.

The threads these individuals have woven and the gifts they shared have had a transformational impact on my life. They have been transformational not only at the time of contact but also in shaping my view of humanity, influencing what matters most to me, my values and how I want to interact with others. They have influenced my worldview and the actions I take in this world to build a future filled with hope and possibility. My mantra—I see you, I celebrate you, you matter!—is the reflection of these beautiful threads in my tapestry of life and how I felt it their presence. They are the beacons of humanity, carrying the hope for a brighter tomorrow.

You may not have Marg, Lorraine and David, Sharon, Felicity, Noula or Glen in your life, but if you still yourself long enough and turn off the noise and distraction around you I'm sure you'll begin to see the lights appear before your eyes. As your eyes begin to adjust and your focusing gaze becomes fixed, you'll be able to see more and more shining, illuminating the spaces around you. The luminescent glow of the special people who not only crossed your path on your journey but weaved a part of who they into the fabric of your life.

There are occasional threads no longer continuing in the tapestry of my life but neither cut off, I'm curious, pondering their meaning, why does the strand stop weaving at that place? Could there be a time in the future when it will to weave back into the story? Only then seeing with clarity the purpose or lesson and feeling grateful it hadn't been knotted and cut off or just left to fray. I celebrate the moments of serendipity and honor all who are a part of my journey.

"Only through our connectedness to others can we really know and enhance self. And only through working on the self can we begin to enhance our connectedness to others."—Harriet Lerner

UBUNTU—The weave of humanity, I am because of who we are. As my life interweaves with yours may we create a rich tapestry, a beautiful and meaningful masterpiece of our shared connectedness and humanity.

Kellie Hackney

H ope is the thread which is woven from the past and into the present; it tells my story of overcoming, triumph and possibility. Hope is found in the stillness and in the knowing. Hope grows through connection and belonging.

Kellie lives with her partner Glen on the beautiful Worimi Country, Port Stephens, on the East Coast of Australia. Kellie works for a small not-for-profit where she leads the organization's family work team.

Kellie loves learning and is a seeker of wisdom and understanding. She loves art and values curiosity and creativity. Kellie loves people—she believes everyone has a place and a purpose, and when they connect with themselves magic happens.

Having left home at fourteen, Kellie completed her HSC whilst living in a refuge with thirteen other girls. Kellie turned eighteen halfway through her first year at university on her way to becoming a teacher. It was in her early twenties when she found she could no longer run from the trauma of her childhood and teens. Kellie's addiction and mental health were sending her life spiraling out of control. She reached out for help and spent nine months at the Teen Challenge Rehab Centre. And in 2000 to 2001 Kellie was fortunate to be accepted into the first dialectical behavior therapy (DBT) trial in Australia. Kellie was on the Disability Support Pension for a number of these years and had received medical reports that she would never work again due her PTSD. Kellie has since engaged in further postgrad studies and worked full-time for the past fourteen years in the community services sector including in leadership positions.

Kellie credits her remarkable recovery to:

- The sacred promise she made to herself decades ago to always look for the light and to always remember it shines the way for hope and possibility.
- The amazing people who have walked with her along this journey.
- Her partner Glen—her biggest cheerleader, hero and friend.
- Her counselors and doctors who not only believed her but also believed *in* her.
- Her wonderful colleagues, both past and present, especially her amazing team who inspire her every day and help so many parents be the best parents they can be.
- Her tribe of friends who have laughed, cried and celebrated with her. Many of whom have welcomed her into their homes and their families.
- And lastly, who she dedicates this chapter to—her sister Jodie, her nieces and nephew. I see you, I celebrate you, you matter!

Trauma changed me, it changed my story, but it didn't end there; in owning my story I found the strength and courage to write my own ending—it's a beautiful story of healing, connecting and belonging.

"Something beautiful, something good. All my confusion He understood, All I had to offer Him was brokenness and strife, but He made something beautiful of my life."
— *"Something Beautiful" by Bill Gaither Trio & Gaither Vocal Band*

ESCAPE TO EMPOWERMENT

A Journey of Healing and Heroes

VIKKI SPELLER

I can't go to Bali, my mum just died! These were the words echoing in my mind.

The thought of leaving after her death felt wrong but part of me wanted so badly to go. It seemed like a way to escape from my sorrows and enjoy life without having any responsibilities. But still, the guilt I felt at leaving home during such an emotionally turbulent time consumed me; how could I possibly go on vacation while everyone else is mourning?

Monica, who has been a close friend since my children's schooling, spoke about Bali and her yoga teacher's retreat, gently suggesting it may be good to get away. I was almost convinced until I heard the words, "We can even go on a bike ride through villages." My heart sank. I hadn't ridden a bike for over thirty years! *No, that's it—I just can't go!*

My mind was in turmoil, I had been plagued with self-doubt, exhaustion and an all-consuming grief from the recent loss of my mother. But oh, how desperately I wanted to run away! To leave everything and everyone behind me; not because I didn't love them, my family are my world, but because the past couple of years had been filled with a combination of hope, pain and sadness. I felt compelled to break free, and Bali sounded so tempting, it was as if my very soul was being led there—or was it my mum?

My mother, Jenny, was an incredible woman, my true hero, and I look back with immense gratitude for everything that she did for me throughout my life. She had a heart of gold, was the life of the party, and I just couldn't believe that she was now gone! Even when she was struggling with her cancer diagnosis, she still found ways to make us all smile.

My mother may have been physically short in stature but in my eyes, she was larger than life. I can still see her face so clearly, her short wavy strawberry-blonde hair, her blue eyes sparkling brightly behind her thin metal glasses and her infectious smile that could light up a room no matter what mood you were in!

It broke my heart watching her slowly die from the disease; it felt like I was losing my best friend just as we were getting to know each other on a deeper level than ever before. I wasn't ready for her to go! I had gotten a full-time job at fourteen and left home at an early age. Growing up, I never truly grasped the magnitude of my mother's role in our family until I became a mother myself. She dedicated her life to us, her four children, and despite the cheekiness of her personality, she took being a mum very seriously. She did her best to be there for us throughout our childhood and schooling years—supporting us in any way she could and encouraging us on our journeys, often shedding tears of pride.

Mum was always strong, determined and mature beyond her years, marrying at the age of sixteen and having completed our family circle just prior to her twenty-fifth birthday. When Mum was diagnosed with cancer, as a family we were devastated; I remember sitting in the doctors' holding Mum's hand as if it were yesterday. But instead of only having a few months to spend with us as suggested, Mum wasn't ready to give up on life just yet, with her brave spirit refusing to let go so easily. From a young age, Mum proved herself strong-willed and determined; despite nearly being lost several times throughout her childhood due to chronic asthma and an appendix attack which she miraculously pulled through.

Mum was steadfast in making the most of her remaining time on earth, ensuring that every moment was filled with as much laughter, joy and love as possible. She set an example to us all by showing strength in the face of adversity, courage in the face of fear, how humor can offer a new perspective and how at times in life sheer stubbornness can serve you well—these were all traits that made my mother truly remarkable.

She taught me many invaluable lessons throughout our lives together, most importantly to cherish every moment spent with family and friends, to be kind and giving even when times are difficult, and above all else, always stay true to yourself no matter what circumstances.

But to me what made Mum even more special is how much she gave back to the community around her. I remember seeing Mum happily volunteering her services wherever possible, nothing was ever too big or small for my mum to tackle with energy and enthusiasm.

She showed me that true strength comes from lending your time and energy into making something bigger than yourself; that giving back can be such a rewarding experience; that you don't need anything materialistic in order to make an impact on someone's life or the world around you and that sometimes just simply being present is enough.

This is something that has stayed with me; it's a philosophy that I have tried to live my life by, that everyone can make a difference if they choose to, no matter their age or circumstances in life. I owe so much of who I am today to this amazing lady whose legacy will live on through myself, my siblings and our children. Mum truly is my hero who has left an imprint on my heart forevermore.

I found Mum's last few weeks to be difficult but also precious; each moment seemed like an eternity yet passed too quickly at the same time. Together as mother and daughter, we talked openly about anything and everything, memories old and new and helped each other make peace with the past. Mum's greatest fear was being forgotten which

I firmly promised could never possibly happen. Mum may have been strong-willed, but she held fragility, full of love for life despite its cruelty sometimes, she was a true source of inspiration for me.

Mum's undeniable courage afforded her with just over two more years with us. I knew the day would come, but even then, it didn't make saying goodbye any easier. We gathered together as family, my hands were softly encircling Mum's left hand, admiring the freckles that seemed to dance upon her skin. As tears streamed down my face, Mum smiled gently one last time before closing her eyes forever, leaving behind a legacy unparalleled in strength, courage and determination. This moment in time is etched into my memory, the pain from the loss of my mum so raw, and yet as each day passed, Monica's words kept floating around in my mind, *Let's go to Bali.*

Was I really willing to jump on a plane and run away? I'd never even been overseas before! Monica and I were both women who always put their families first. I was a devoted wife and mother to my three wonderful children, but lately I felt like an empty shell of myself, as if no matter how much effort I put in, nothing seemed to fill that void inside me. My life felt like it was on autopilot and I was just going through the motions, without any real purpose or joy in my days. I missed my mum terribly and I missed ME.

Despite all the doubts in my head telling me not to go, my need to escape and Monica's enthusiasm eventually won out and we booked our tickets with me silently beckoning Mum's spirit to join us on our adventure.

As I boarded the plane and felt the energy of excitement envelop me, a sense of relief began to wash over me. I was ready to experience all Bali had to offer, except for the bike ride! I had adamantly insisted under no circumstances would I be riding a bike in Bali!

From the moment I stepped off the plane and into Bali's warm embrace, I knew this place held something special for me. The resort villa was nothing short of breathtaking. Its high ceilings seemed to soar up into the sky and each morning began with a freshly cut coconut and colorful fruit whose flavors tantalised the taste buds.

This magical island called Bali spoke to me like no other place before. Everywhere I looked there were reminders of its beauty—sacred temples, tropical mountains and cascading waterfalls. Every day presented new experiences, from trekking through lush rice fields to sipping tea overlooking volcanic hillsides. With each night ending under a blanket of stars as I showered beneath the moonlight surrounded by nature's orchestra playing softly in the background. And oh, how Monica and I laughed, deep belly laughs that caused tears to roll down cheeks, leaving us unable to stop even if we wanted to.

I felt Bali's spiritual heartbeat had connected to mine and was healing me from the inside out. All the while in the back of my mind was the thought of the ever-looming bike ride which was scheduled for the day before we were to leave, and Monica's kind words of encouragement to have faith in myself and my abilities.

Well, it was inevitable, the moment I had been dreading had arrived. My heart raced and my stomach churned. All around me the other women from the retreat were choosing their bikes with excitement and anticipation. All I could feel was fear; after all, it had been years since I'd even ridden a bike!

I can't do this! I'm going to fall off, it's too dangerous, and it's so far! My mind was in overdrive. What had happened to me? I used to be so optimistic and confident. It was like all my anxiety, grief and fears around losing my mother had been channeled into whether I could ride a bike or not! What was my mind doing? I did my best to muster up some courage despite my anxiety, as there was something inside me saying this was an opportunity not to be missed.

Monica casually tucked her long blonde hair under her bike helmet, encouraging me to start by picking a bike to see how I feel. Taking a deep breath, I reluctantly chose one of the bikes but it didn't feel safe, so I decided to give it back to the tour guide. I picked another, trying it for good measure, but it didn't feel right either. The tour guide gave me a genuine smile of understanding, finding me a bike he thought would suit. It was the right height and looked newer which gave me some sense of security. I nervously straddled the bike and started to pedal, wobbling around like a child first learning to walk. It felt strange to be on a bike after so many years but also strangely familiar, as a wave of courage washed over me; *Maybe I can actually do this?*

The group eagerly headed off while I was still clumsily and tentatively doing my best to coordinate my pedaling, steering and balance, feeling self-conscious and embarrassed at my lack of bike-riding skills.

Monica offered to stay alongside me as her tall lean body looked naturally confident riding along the road. I was grateful for her company as she could have easily ridden ahead with the rest of the women. We slowly made our way, stopping off to meet a Balinese family who opened up their home for us, bringing awareness to their culture and lifestyle. A brief reprieve from the torture I perceived to be putting myself through, but soon we were on our way once more. I felt that familiar rush as my heart began to pound faster with anticipation, as if echoing my innermost thoughts. I felt a tinge of guilt as Monica continued to stay by my side. Not wanting to take away from her experience, I let her know I was feeling more confident and to ride ahead. Truth be known, I wasn't! I continued to concentrate on staying upright on the bike, dodging potholes, rocks and the occasional car wondering what was I thinking! I would much rather be having a massage right now!

This was when it hit me … that right here and now I had a choice to make—one between embracing this experience fully or continuing to be a prisoner to my fears. In that moment everything changed. With every passing second more courage filled me up until eventually, I found myself feeling relaxed and gaining confidence, no longer needing to concern myself with trying to stay upright but instead enjoying every twist and turn along the way. While drinking in the breathtaking views that surrounded me, I had found my rhythm, let go of my fears and become fully present.

As I rode past the endless rice fields, memories from my childhood flooded into my mind's eye, which was both joyous and painful, but even still, I felt strangely at peace. As I looked ahead to the long stretch of road that lay before me, something unexpected happened—out of nowhere I felt my mum with me. Her love washing over me like a wave of warmth that radiated through every cell in my body. I felt her pride for my courage to travel overseas, facing my fears and for releasing the limiting beliefs I had placed upon myself.

With each pedal forward that feeling grew stronger until finally it felt almost tangible, like she was actually riding alongside me. In an instant, I saw a vision of Mum's smiling face so clearly in front of me that it almost took my breath away. Her voice seemed to come from everywhere, gentle yet clearly audible, saying, "*I love you, sweetheart. I'm so happy we came here.*" Tears streaming down my face, I rode on through every sobbing gasp for air as all the pent-up emotions from the past two years just poured out of me like a tsunami.

The air blowing past my face felt freeing, washing away my pain, the sun shining down upon me was fueling my heart, filling me with hope and optimism once more until eventually there were no more tears to shed but instead a sense of pure happiness as I felt Mum riding along with me. Enjoying the experience of life through me!

This was a blessed reminder that we are never alone. Our ancestors who have gone before us and those yet to come will be there with love and encouragement—pulling us forward, offering strength during times of despair or celebration when success is ours. You stand at a sacred point—between past and future generations—safe within their spiritual embrace as they recognize your journey from this world until eternity! It was in this moment that the spirit of my mother was there for me, enveloping me in the essence of her love.

I was the last rider back that day with the final leg being an uphill challenge to our destination. With determination, I kept pedaling, smiling, pushing myself forward with a sense of pride and accomplishment. I was hot, sweaty, physically and emotionally exhausted, but I made it! With the women from the retreat being incredibly welcoming, especially my dear friend Monica who had offered me so much love and support.

I realised then how much we can miss when we don't embrace life's opportunities head-on, not just physically but mentally and emotionally too! By taking risks outside our comfort zone, we open ourselves up to discovering so many amazing things life has to offer us if only we have faith enough to try them out!

It turned out my greatest fear and biggest excuse for not wanting to attend my overseas retreat would instead be the most profoundly healing experience, shaping my future of stepping even greater into my career of supporting people in embracing themselves, finding their voice and choosing courage over fear enabling them to experience some truly incredible things! I felt the depths of all emotions while in Bali; for me it was a place of deep healing, spiritual growth and pure joy. A moment that I will carry in my heart forever.

I hold deep gratitude for Monica's friendship and the experience we shared on our 2014 overseas adventure. Monica was my hero when I needed one and Bali was too!

As we journey through life, many heroes are placed before us, some at the time we don't recognise as heroes until the lessons of life unfold and we look back and reflect on a moment in time; like the young boy behind the counter offering you a genuine smile on a day where everything seems to be going wrong, or the older woman at the clothing store granting wise advice from her life's experiences; or that brief moment when asked by a stranger "How are you?" and they listen with an empathic ear and an open heart, fully present, while the busyness of life swirls around you. These are our unsung heroes enriching our lives with their compassion and understanding.

Heroes, whether fleeting as they pass through life in a moment, or as family or friends that walk alongside us, sharing the journey of our lives, or those in spirit supporting us, they are all equally as magnificent and brilliant.

There is a hero that lies deep within all of us, that brave inner voice that guides us through even the most challenging moments and encourages us to pursue our hopes and dreams in the face of fear. Having this courage ripples out and shows those around us that they too can be courageous, they too can achieve their wishes. With this inner strength we're reminded of the incredible potential within each one of us!

In turn, you are someone's hero. You may have been a hero for them without you even realising it, like Monica was for me, but I can promise that you have changed someone's life in ways you may never understand. So, as we journey through life, let us dedicate ourselves to empowering each other and being heroes for one another as well as ourselves! And in those moments where you feel you have nothing left to give, be open to receiving a hero in your life and allow them the gift of showing up for you!

Vikki Speller

Vikki Speller is a highly respected intuitive life coach, holistic counselor and women's circle and retreat facilitator, who embraces her calling to guide others towards their soul purpose. Since 2008, Vikki has stood firmly in this transformative space with a passion for empowering individuals, nurturing self-love and honoring intuition, and has become a beacon of inspiration and spiritual wisdom.

Vikki has immersed herself in the field of spirituality and wellness. Approaching her coaching practice with compassion, empathy and a genuine desire to uplift and support individuals on their unique paths. Drawing on her intuitive abilities, energy healing and holistic counseling background, Vikki empowers people to tap into their inner strength, make aligned decisions and manifest their dreams. Through one-on-one coaching sessions, in person or online, and as a certified meditation and mindfulness teacher, she provides a safe and nurturing space for clients to explore their authentic selves, discover their passions and overcome obstacles.

As a women's intuitive coach, Vikki has impacted the lives of countless individuals, both in person and through her online platform, creating a ripple effect of transformation that spans the globe. With a compassionate heart and drawing upon her own life experiences, she has a deep understanding of the challenges women face, guiding her clients on a journey to connect with their intuition, find their courage and unlock their inner wisdom.

Through her holistic approach, as a women's circle facilitator, Vikki creates safe and nurturing spaces for women to come together, share their stories and support one another. These circles offer a sanctuary where women can explore their authentic selves, heal wounds and cultivate a sense of community. Through her facilitation, Vikki fosters deep connections, providing transformative experiences that enable women to grow and thrive, empowering them to live authentic lives filled with purpose and self-love.

Vikki's dedication to creating positive change extends beyond her work with adults. Recognising the immense importance of nurturing children's emotional well-being and self-acceptance, she has become a passionate advocate for empowering young minds, having had experience working as a qualified child care educator and also within the education system.

As an author, Vikki has an array of diverse offerings including her enchanting children's books, where she weaves tales that inspire self-love, instil a positive mindset and encourage the practice of mindfulness and affirmations. Also providing children's card packs, each designed to uplift and guide young souls on their path to self-acceptance and compassion for others.

Vikki is deeply passionate about nurturing children and adults alike in holding a strong sense of self offering her range of captivating oracle cards and affirmation card sets, and her upcoming spiritual self-help series of books holds the promise of connecting readers to the profound wisdom of the spiritual realm, as she channels messages of insight and guidance.

Vikki lives on the Sunshine Coast in Queensland, Australia, with her husband and treasures making memories with family, spending quality time with her three grown-up children and beautiful little granddaughter. As Vikki's journey continues to unfold, she invites us to embark on our own, knowing that within each of us lies an infinite capacity for growth, wisdom and the power to create a life filled with purpose and joy.

Website: vikkispeller.com
Instagram: @vikki_speller_intuition_plus
Facebook: Intuition Plus

DEEP DIVES, SEA BREEZES & FLOATING IN LAGOONS

MIRANDA MURRAY

Ahhhh Carol … Mrs Spence. Mirmaid #1 *(deliberately misspelt as it's a play on my nickname Mir)*. The sunrise to my tequila. The Frenchie to my Sandy *(GREASE movie fans will get me)*. My partner in crime. My confidante. My supporter. My sounding board. My cheerleader. My shoulder to cry on. My ultimate safe place to land. My instant grounding. My sanctuary. My inspiration. The other spoke of "team glam" beside me on the bicycle. My naughty influence and my reality checker. My get out of jail free card. My friend. My sister from another mister. My soulmate.

Before I met Carol, in many ways I was blind … or perhaps naive is a better term, a little green around the gills, unaware at the tender age of twenty-two that a soulmate could be anything other than that of the romantic kind; the swooning, sweep-you-off-your-feet, love-at-first-sight type that I had seen in movies. I could not have predicted what lay ahead and how much of a monumental impact this quietly spoken, unassuming, graceful, black-haired beauty, who greeted me with her signature, welcoming smile that lit up her whole face, would have on me when I first stepped through the doors into the Club Med New Zealand office boutique in Shortland Street, Auckland, NZ. I was there, no doubt a little nervous, but most definitely curious and keen to find out more about the job that was advertised for the junior position in the company. My first *ever* interview and apparently I must have had beginner's luck—I got the job!

I was not entirely sure exactly what Carol saw in me that day, being less qualified than the role sought out, but the reflections she has shared with me since were that she just "knew" that I would make a great addition to the team, and the rest I could learn. And that was that!

We quickly gelled, along with our beautiful, larger than life colleague, Tracey, with her wicked laugh and killer keyboard skills. We spent long hours in our little office boutique, which affectionately came to be known as "The Bitt-a-que" or "The fishbowl". This was due to its expansive glass windows, wrapped around its semicircular exterior, showcasing the brightly lit, tropical holiday feel of the interior decor that lay within. Daily videos played on the TV screen, displaying seductive images of the beautiful Club Med resorts around the world. Its lure, enticing tired CBD workers into our office suite, to pick up brochures and wistfully dream of faraway destinations, as they trudged past on their lunchbreaks.

I was fresh out of university, in fact I still had a few subjects to complete my tertiary education degree, which ended up taking me another fourteen years to return to, once I'd sailed through those tropical doors that day, but that's a story for another time. Two weeks later I found myself floating in a lagoon on the tropical island of Mo'orea in Tahiti. Carol had whisked me off to experience a Club Med resort for myself, to live and breathe the product we were selling and to help her with a large conference group she was looking after. As I floated on my back in the clear blue waters of that Mo'orean lagoon and glanced back at the white sandy beach, dotted with coconut palms and blissfully happy holidaymakers lazing in pool loungers as they sipped delicious cocktails, I thought, *Well … this working gig is alright.* Haha. It was a long way from the life of a uni student that I'd been living a mere two weeks prior to that, and it was the experience of a lifetime right off the bat. I had landed my dream job!

We worked hard and played equally hard in our downtime. I quickly learnt so much about working life, sometimes by being thrown in the deep end. Early on I had to escort another large group all on my own, due to unforeseen circumstances preventing Carol from traveling with them. Again, she saw something in me that I was yet to see. With unwavering faith, Carol sent me off on my next big adventure, solely in charge, with a serious amount of duty of care for our precious clients, with the confidence that I would do a stellar job. At least that is what she led me to believe. To this day, I'm not sure if she actually did feel confident, or if she simply knew how important it would be for me to think that she trusted that I was fully capable. Her encouragement and gesture of the trust she had in me, catapulted me into an opportunity that I possibly would not have ever put my hand up for, at such a fledgling stage in my career.

Those moments of Carol taking a chance on me lead to so much rapid personal and professional growth which I consider to be a foundational part of my approach to work and life now as I near the end of my forties. With that trust and connection, our working relationship swiftly became a friendship and then like family. The seal on our bubble of confidence—watertight. Whilst I am closer in age to Carol's children, there is an undeniable connection that we share and as the years have whizzed by, I now find myself at a similar age to that which Carol was when she first employed me. I too find myself in positions of extending my hand to younger women and inviting them to stand on my shoulders to support them on their journey. What an incredible role model Carol has been. Twenty-seven years have passed since that day we met, and we are still BFFs now, our bond ever more strengthened by the experiences and adventures we have shared, the tears we have shed, the celebrations we have toasted to and always an abundance of laughter and love together.

I am forever grateful to Carol for helping to pave the way forward for me from that young age, and in fact, it is she whom I must thank, in part, for my beautiful little family. As I was regaining perspective on life and reemerging into the world again after seven non-viable fertility treatments and the subsequent breakdown and divorce of my first marriage, it was *her* crazy idea that we embark on a huge fundraising adventure together. On opposite sides of the Tasman from each other, we bought bikes, trained for a year, donned Lycra and joined forty-six other like-minded souls on an "800kms in 8 days" fundraising bicycle ride across Thailand, from Bangkok to Khao Lak, raising money for an Australian run charity organization called "Hands Across The Water", which supports much-needed homes and community projects for at-risk children in Thailand.

It was there on that ride in 2014, where I met my second soul mate, Daniel, who is now my husband. The kids in the homes we support became mine and Dan's first family together, cementing a bond like no other and just under three years later, we eloped up to one of the homes called "Home Hug" and shared our secret nuptials with the children and beautiful staff we love so much, in a little town called Yasothon in the far north-east Isaan region. That place, those incredible humans—they all had us at hello and we couldn't imagine doing it any other way. We journeyed on from there to Barcelona on our honeymoon, where we had our fourth and final fertility treatment together and came home pregnant with our little girl Zoe, who is now almost six years old. Love in Lycra—I tell ya—it's totally a thing!

And all thanks to Carol for enticing me along with her to achieve our big, hairy audacious goal! I agreed because first of all, why wouldn't I want to do something so amazing with my BFF?! And secondly, I knew that if I could set my mind to it, train, fundraise the AU$10,000 and ride 800km in eight days across the dusty, hot roads of Thailand, then I could face and overcome any other challenges that came my way and achieve anything I wanted to in life from that point forward. It was more than just a bike ride, it was another pivotal stage in my life and a fundamentally huge part of me finding my place in the world again and feeling of value amongst a new community of amazing humans.

BOBBING ALONG IN A SEA OF CHANGE

Deb. My unexpected lifeboat who kept me afloat when I was lost in a sea of grief, confusion, overwhelm and doubt, and kept me from disappearing beneath the murky waters at a time when it would have been easy to get washed away.

Not long after the seventh non-viable IVF treatment, my fertility specialists told me I needed to give my body a break before I broke it. My ex-husband and I had endured seven treatment cycles in two years and I was exhausted, we both were. The roller coaster of hope, excitement, disappointment, fear and grief is something that I would not wish on my worst enemy *(not that I have one, but if I did, I wouldn't)*. It's a cruel process at times. I still managed to find a silver lining … the fog slowly lifted a bit and I went back to work, having given it up to try and alleviate some of the stress while we were trying to conceive. But the idea of having a little office banter again excited me, after probably in hindsight too much idle time on my hands at home, with only the dogs to talk to and a full calendar of doctors' appointments, blood tests and schedules for pumping myself full of hormones with the daily injections.

A few months into my new temporary work gig, I sought out some support in finding out what I wanted to do career-wise again. A girlfriend suggested I reach out to a friend of hers who I had hit it off with whilst seated at the same table at her recent wedding.

Enter stage right—Deb—the life coach. A beautiful, confident, self-assured woman whose niche was actually helping parents and teens, but true to Deb's nature, she generously took my call and agreed to book in a session and see if there was some way she could help me, and if not, offered to refer me on to a more suitable colleague.

Likewise with Carol, Deb and I felt like a great fit right from the start, like a favorite hoodie that feels like an instant warm hug when you slide your head and arms through its holes and offers an allowance to show up exactly as you are, with zero expectation of presenting in any particular polished shape or form. We embarked on a series of sessions together with the goal to unpack what it was that I wanted to do next for work. Deb was easy to speak with, supportive and kind, with a willing ear and some great exercises that gave me much food for thought about my working life.

Three sessions in, I sunk down into the familiar nurturing safety of her soft couch, and as she asked how I was, I paused. When I eventually did speak, in a calm and even breath, I told her I had been better and that I was pretty sure my marriage had just fallen apart on the weekend. Somehow, suddenly, my reality had slid like an avalanche, from finding my purpose of work, to struggling to even find which way was up. It was a difficult time!

Some days I cried, some days I just let a verbal waterfall of jumbled thoughts and overwhelm tumble out of my head and mouth and spill onto the floor, the couch, the walls of Deb's office. A couple of times, we booked an extra hour just so I could get it all out. My sessions had instantly stopped being about work that day and instead became about surviving, understanding, feeling heard, seen and at times just sane. And somewhere over the next six months, I healed. I realigned, revived, reconnected to myself and the white noise quietened, the curtains blew gently in the breeze allowing some light back in around my edges. And I peacefully walked through the light at the end of the tunnel and the darkest of nights became brighter days again. I slowly felt myself return, not the same, changed, but able to breathe with more ease and able to focus on my future.

With that came a realization that in fact I wanted to become a life coach!

When I shared this dawning moment with Deb and said, "I think I'd be pretty good at that." She smiled a broad grin, her face beaming and replied, "I could have told you that in about the second session, but you had to get there yourself." To this day, I will never forget that moment, nor those sessions, nor the incredibly safe space that Deb held for me during some of my darkest days. Without a doubt she has helped to carve out a part of who I am today, as this woman who nears her half century, comfortable in my own skin, with a fierce desire to help other women to feel as supported as I did all those months sitting in Deb's beautiful chair, cocooned in her gentle care. Not once did I feel judged, not once did I feel alone.

Deb was ten years older than me, she had changed careers at my age, she too had been through a divorce at my age and here she was thriving, glowing, living her best life full of love, laughter and so many fabulous moments.

Call it divine timing, a gift from the gods, pure luck, serendipity or whatever you will, but Deb coming into my life at that precise time when I needed someone like her, is not something that I take for granted— *ever*. I feel very blessed and grateful.

At the beginning of our sessions, I had thought perhaps my head was considering whether counseling might be where my career goals lay. But having experienced the benefits firsthand of how coaching can help to acknowledge the layers of "stuff" that had brought me to my current situation, I did not want to sit there in the sludge forever. I wanted to take stock, to heal, to grow, to make plans, to take action and to move forwards, towards something more soul expanding, more heartwarming and to feel alive again.

If I hadn't met Deb then, who knows whether I would be where I am today, doing what I do. It's hard to say because I feel like my women's work is such a fundamental part of who I am and maybe I would have found my way here on a different timeline via a different route.

But I can hand on heart say that because of Deb, I became a coach, and my work just continues to evolve and unfold in the most beautiful, natural, easeful way, full of peaceful flow and alignment because she allowed me to stand on her shoulders.

This body has fought a long battle to create my family, it has carried me through some extreme traumas and triumphed over some incredible adventures, both of which I could never have predicted that it would have faced and tackled. None of which I could have navigated alone without these two women and many other beautiful people in my life.

My little girl reflects back to me the way that I love myself these days, my whole, slightly more rounded, softer, more feminine version of me. In the middle of the night when she crawls into our bed like a stealthy ninja of the night, or in moments of illness, worry or just general everyday preschooler life, Zoe seeks comfort amongst my new curves. Her little fingers lovingly trace my smile lines, tug on the less elastic skin of my neck and poke and prod my womanly shape. She gently whispers "more cuddles" as she snuggles into her happy place. It is there that she feels safe, nestled into the squishy, ample bosom that she knows so well.

I love this place where I am at, not just for me but for her as well. I love that I am modeling a body and soul-loving way of being for our little empowered woman.

This chapter is another opportunity to practice all that I have learned,
to come home to myself again,
to embrace all that I am,
and all that I am yet to become,
by gracefully accepting where I am at on this journey of womanhood,
and allowing myself to walk that path at the speed and direction I need to,
without judgment or preconceived ideas of what should be,
how I should look.
These days, my inhales are deep and full, my exhales are long and cleansing.

There is no quickening of breath, shallow catching in my chest and throat.

At peace in this body, this life I have created.

And so very grateful.

I wish this for you too and every woman.

May you find your Carol, your Deb and embrace all that they have shared with you.

Miranda Murray

Miranda believes that now more than ever people are craving connection and understanding. Through her own unique experiences, it has become her life's work to support and empower women, their families and communities to be healthy, happy and to thrive, to always feel like they are enough and to never feel alone.

She has felt first hand the benefits of some truly pivotal moments in her life, where she has been given the opportunity to stand on the shoulders of other beautiful women who have paved the way before her. Their generosity of love, time and genuine authenticity has helped to empower her through challenges, to blossom with new growth and has been the catalyst for so much positive change along her path. It is thanks in part to them, that she has developed such a strong self-awareness and connection with her identity that lies at the core of her being, and the ability to recognize that familiar feeling of warmth when a flame of inspiration, alignment and "calling" is ignited in her belly, reminding her of her place in this world.

Miranda wished this very gift for every other woman and her deepest desire is to continue to pay it forward by empowering other women in the same way in which she, herself has been empowered.

Her own journey through the sudden loss of her mother as a young child, her struggle to become one herself in her adult years, the breakdown of her first marriage, the birth of not only a new chapter that saw a new adventure, a new purpose, a new love, and eventually the arrival of her daughter who her second husband and she welcomed into their family in 2017.

Miranda can credit so many soulful women who made their mark on her "big ole bruised heart" along the way, both young and old.

And now, she helps support women and their families through Coaching, Speaking, Workshops, Women's Circles, Social and Business events. She is excited to be adding as much value as she can to her local community and beyond.

These beautiful gatherings have enabled Miranda to support more women, and to share with others the absolute value that can be found in the shared wisdom amongst the women in our communities. Miranda believes that every woman should be given the opportunity to experience the magic that happens when women come together in this way.

And she feels that when people feel heard, seen, and understood, there is a greater opportunity for positive solutions and outcomes in all areas of their lives.

Miranda is so driven to be part of that change for good and help others to build a life where not only can they feel happier, but they can feel proud of the meaningful connections and contributions they make.

Miranda and her husband, Daniel, co-founded their family-run business Empathic Consulting Pty Ltd, just before their little girl was born. They believe empathy is the most important capability to create improved outcomes for individuals, for families, for businesses, for leaders and for communities. While too often ignored or misunderstood, empathy is the capacity for a person to understand the rational and emotional drivers of others.

They are on a mission to change the world so there is more of this out there for the future of their daughter and all the other children to grow up in; a world of deeper connection, community, humanity that is based on support, trust and understanding.

Volunteering and contributing to the great work that some Australian not-for-profits do is a core part of the Murray family values with a few being their main current focus: Hands Across The Water who supports at risk children and communities in Thailand to have a life of choice, not chance, Feel the Magic® who provides grief education and support to bereaved children and their families to help alleviate the pain and isolation felt by the loss of a parent, sibling, or legal guardian. Having lost her Mum at 6 years old, Miranda can appreciate the value personally of children who are experiencing grief, being supported to reach their full potential. She also volunteers with In Great Company who connects social carers with elderly people living at home through visits to alleviate their feelings of loneliness and isolation. We all need support at both bookends of our life and the bits in between.

Miranda is honoured to be a part of this next beautiful anthology *Ubuntu* which reflects her values, philosophy, and the way she lives her life, in alignment with all that she holds true to her, in supporting women, their families and communities to thrive together.

I AM A REFLECTION OF THOSE WHO LIFTED ME UP

JUDY CHEUNG-WOOD

When I started immersing myself in the role as a leader of my growing my brand, SkinB5, and being responsible for inspiring my team members every day, I put more intent into sharpening my ability to take on feedback, self-reflection and become more aware of who I am and my purpose in this lifetime.

I used to be told that "you are unpredictable"—which was feedback that I never truly understood because in my mind I am very consistent, I was very focused on working out how to get to my "vision goal". As I reflect on this feedback and observe how I live my life, only now many years later have I started to understand where my "unpredictability" came from.

I live serendipitously most of the time, as I keep my mind and heart open, dreaming about possibilities and discovering the magic of life, one heartstring tug at a time. This is how I came to be part of this anthology, *Ubuntu*.

When Dr Tererai Trent reached out to me to make sure that I was still keen on sharing my story in her new anthology, I told her I was very excited and honored to be in her new book, but I was not sure if I understood the true deeper meaning of the word ubuntu. You see, before

I commit to doing something, I need to know that I understand the meaning of it.

One night, I was just flicking through Netflix programs and had no idea what I wanted to watch. I came across a docuseries called *The Playbook*. The title of the first episode: "Doc Rivers: A Coach's Rules for Life". I had no idea who Doc Rivers was, but thought, *Perhaps I can learn some leadership lessons from an American professional basketball player and coach!* As the story progressed, it went on to explain what inspired Doc Rivers to change his tact with the players of the Boston Celtics, which ultimately led the team to a National Basketball Association (NBA) championship in 2008. The program went on to explain how Doc Rivers' success was sparked by the ancient African word ubuntu meaning "humanity to others" or often described as reminding us that "I am what I am because of who we all are".

I felt goosebumps. That was it, my story will be in Dr Tererai Trent's *Ubuntu* anthology!

So here I am. But what am I supposed to write about? Tererai said, "It's about honoring and celebrating the heroines who paved the path to their dreams. Think about a time when you faced the worst circumstances in your life, the situation that almost derailed your dream, and the individual/s who helped you navigate to achieve your dreams."

One of my dreams was to become an author, but I had no idea how I was going to do that! However, through winning three AusMumpreneur 2021 awards, I had the opportunity to participate in the *Sacred Promise* anthology project. I was very much drawn by Peace, Katy, Karen and Tererai's shared vision to help improve the lives of other women and young girls across the world. And, here I am while in the process of writing for my second and third book in two years.

So, firstly, I wanted to honor in this book, Peace, Katy, Karen and Tererai for helping me get to my dream to become an author. I have the opportunity to share my story here with you, because I am able to stand on the shoulders of these incredible women.

But my loftiest dream was always to run my own successful business, ever since I was a child, and I loved playing trade.

A friend of mine of Indian heritage once told me that we evolve through four stages of life. As I reflect on the significant people in my life who have helped lift me up through life's treacherous mountain paths and the associated epic battles within, I cannot help but think of those who have acted in the most pivotal ways in my life, which ultimately prepared me to be worthy of my dreams.

MY CHILDHOOD

My mother always told me that one day when I become a mother myself, I would understand why she did certain things—she was very strict with us and she firmly believed in physical discipline which was very common amongst Asian families back then. We feared her. You see, my grandfather used to discipline his twelve children the same way, typically with a small cane about two feet long that was designed to leave long parallel welts on arms and legs as painful reminders of the consequences of bad behavior.

Because I was a boisterous child, and my sister was my partner in crime, I have so many vivid memories of Mum chasing after us with a cane. One of those memories was while we were growing up in Honiara in the Solomon Islands.

As I mentioned in my chapter in the *Sacred Promise* book, I had an unusual but magical upbringing in the Solomon Islands. My parents ran a general store, like a mini department store, selling everything from food and snacks, to fishing equipment and clothing. My sister and I were obsessed with the Wrigley Juicy Fruit chewing gum.

One night when the store was closed and our parents went to bed, my sister and I snuck into the store and took boxes of Juicy Fruit. Of course, Mum noticed the missing boxes the next day, and we denied taking them! "Lies!" She eventually found the boxes stashed under our beds and all hell broke loose.

This time my sister and I were determined to hide from her cane, so we ended up under the house where excess stock was stored. I hid in a corner and heard my sister climbing into what sounded like a cardboard box. We stayed there for hours and hours, the whole time we could hear my Mum's heavy footsteps stomping up and down the wooden floorboards above us and shouting our names!

Eventually, I came out to face my judgment, but my sister stayed hidden. Hours after I handed myself in, there was still no sign of my sister. My Mum started to panic as it was now nighttime—she is missing! I didn't want to betray my sister but I too started to worry about her safety, so I led Mum and my maternal grandparents who lived with us at the time to the dark storage area under the house where they found her sound asleep inside a tall cardboard box.

We didn't get the cane (what?!), because my maternal grandmother told my mother to back off.

My maternal grandmother (her name was Ying, and we grandchildren called her Popo), was my inspiration and anchor during my childhood. I looked up and listened to her closely. She was always smiley, warm, engaging, loving, centered, insightful and full of wisdom—I could easily use many more fabulous words to describe her! She was always the clearheaded, street-smart figure in the family who was able to instantly see through people and situations. She was always spot-on with her warnings and advice.

I realise now that the wisdom my Popo imparted on me has laid the strongest foundation in my personal belief and value systems that keep me firmly centered and grounded, particularly in times of challenges and distress.

Popo's loving and generous approach made me feel valued and understood. When I think of her, I remember her super warm hands cupping mine as she shared her wise thoughts to help us understand situations better, why my mum acted the way she did, and why people behaved a certain way. One of those wisdoms that stuck with me was to "never believe in what a person says, but observe how they act when they think no one is watching". A timeless piece of wisdom, indeed, which I apply in my life often.

While Popo nurtured us emotionally, my maternal grandfather (his name was Fung, and we called him Gung-gung) nurtured us intellectually. Gung-gung was born in 1920 in Guangzhou, a southern province in China. He was a very progressive and intelligent person.

He was a chemist who graduated from a university in Hong Kong. Back in those days this was equivalent to getting a PhD, when most people in China at best would achieve only secondary education with most having to join the workforce to support their families after primary school education, including my own mother.

Because my mother was very close to my grandparents, I count myself very lucky to have had the opportunity to live with him during my childhood years. Gung-gung was a man of many talents. People referred to him as "The Scientist" because he used to manufacture excellent skin and hair care products that everyone swears by. He was also an accomplished artist with a passion for Chinese watercolor painting—I cherish my small but precious collection that he gave me. He wrote poems; he was a calligrapher too. Above all, he was a lifelong entrepreneur. Throughout his working life he had a grocery store, restaurant, manufactured skin care products, made wooden toys and even had an advertising agency! I still have some of his scrapbooks where he kept all his business ideas and clippings for inspiration—his version of a Pinterest account! He fast filled his big A3 scrapbooks all the way up until he passed away at the age of ninety-eight.

My mum told me recently, when we saw on a program that talked about hand-painted advertising posters that, "Your Gung-gung used to do that for brands after the war!"

Wow, I was mesmerised. There are still so many things to discover about him!

I believe that my grandmother's essence lives on with me, and my grandfather's entrepreneurial, progressive, open-minded and lifelong learning spirit has shaped who I am today. Together, they have given me the strongest foundation to enable me to become an innovative and ethical entrepreneur.

MY TEENAGE YEARS

We all inevitably come to the realisation that life is never a straight, even road. As I have shared in the *Sacred Promise* book, my earlier life in the Solomon Islands was magical, then it all came crashing down and my childhood was seriously interrupted.

My parents took us to Macau and left my sister and me at a boarding school run by Catholic nuns while they dealt with "some troubles" that my father had gotten into. Those years were scarring for both my sister and me. We reunited after eighteen months and moved back to Hong Kong.

In the few years that followed, I became a quiet, studious teenager, but I was rebellious at the same time. I felt different because I had a very different childhood compared to everyone else and it was hard for me to emotionally fit in with my peers. When I was eleven years old, one night around midnight, my dad woke my sister and me up, telling us he had to leave *now* for an urgent overseas business trip. He never returned.

The few years after he left were difficult for my mum, now a single mother. My mother has every reason to resent my father for losing all our family fortunes, those she had earned through the entrepreneurial and hardworking spirit she'd learnt from her father. I know she resented him, because she told us so many times over. But one thing she did reinforce to us was that she would allow us to have a relationship with my father if we wanted it. In the end, we chose not to because we gave him every opportunity to make things right with my mother but he chose not to correct his wrongs.

One day, soon after I turned sixteen, my mum asked, "Do you want to go overseas to study?" Without hesitation, I replied excitedly, "YES!" At the time, one of my aunties had just immigrated to New Zealand. My mum made arrangements with her, then the next thing I knew I was applying for a student visa. I remember feeling determined to embark on a new chapter in my life. It was a very emotional occasion, having to say goodbye to my close friends, Mum and sister at the Hong Kong airport. I asked my trusted friends to look after my mother and sister for me.

Before I knew it, I'd arrived in Auckland, New Zealand. I cried the first six months after arriving every time my mum and sister called. I would not see them again for the next four years because plane tickets were so expensive and we couldn't afford it when my mum was paying expensive international student school fees.

I settled in well in New Zealand and made good friends. Living with my auntie, uncle and four cousins was easy because they were very kind, made me feel so welcomed and looked after me very generously. When they built a new house, they even set aside a room for me, all to myself! It meant the world to me.

A few gifts and "thank you" would never be able to express the depth of my gratitude for their generosity and kindness. My amazing experience in New Zealand would provide me with the strength I needed to start developing into the independent, resourceful and adaptive person who would be capable of achieving my dreams.

In fact, I became "too independent", my mother said. At times, she would tell me that perhaps she should have kept me by her side instead. I understand now, as a mother, what she meant by that. She sacrificed a lot emotionally in order to place me on a path of possibilities to get to where I am today—none of what I have achieved to date would have been possible without her "letting me go".

MY ADULTHOOD

Looking back, I was a bit of a lost soul during my earlier adulthood. I was very restless, and I did a lot of things to keep myself occupied—hobby classes, yoga, pilates, gym, working many all-nighters, going out with friends sometimes into the wee hours in the morning.

But even, as one of my team leaders at work put it at the time, "burning your candle at both ends", I still felt empty spiritually. Only when I had some rare alone time, like riding on the bus or train or walking home, would I start to think about why I felt so lost and rudderless.

On the surface, I came across as someone who was very focused on advancing my career upwards as a highly competent urban planning professional who was working for the largest clients in the country, the likes of Woolworths, BP, Multiplex, Stockland, Lendlease etc.

Spiritually, I was in no-man's-land until my early thirties. And as time went on it was slowly eating me away—it started to affect my ability to handle pressures at work and caused discontentment and clashes in my close relationships.

Then, I had an epiphany to develop a nutraceutical range to treat problematic skin based on my newfound personal experience with dietary supplements that unexpectedly cleared up my skin—I had struggled with ongoing skin breakouts since I was twelve years old.

I shared with my partner at the time, "I think this is what I want to do." I don't recall if he responded to me, but I do remember that he didn't like the idea, as it was not a secure and stable career path.

I secretly worked on my idea, and a number of months later, I abruptly announced that I was giving up my promising urban planning career that I'd worked so hard for, and told my partner of ten years that it wasn't working out between us. Just like that, I walked away from everything I knew.

THE REST IS HISTORY

Fast-forward to today, I am happily married, have a wonderful daughter, my global skin care business is flourishing and helping thousands of people with troubled skin. I am well and truly on track to reaching my dreams.

There are so many people who helped me get here, one small act at a time, whether they know it or not. I learnt that even bad experiences and failures were part of the journey that meant I had to prepare, and they would guide me to where I needed to go. So I thanked everyone, friends or foe, with whom I crossed paths along the way.

But there is one person that I want to particularly honor in this *Ubuntu* anthology, and that is my husband, Jason.

Most people when they first meet us think we are an odd-looking pair, as we don't fit with who they imagined our other half to be.

I met Jason at a time of my life where I was on the verge of "losing my marbles". My skin care business was not going well, I was constantly fighting with my then business partners, my personal relationships were either a mess or empty spiritually, my family thought I was making some really bad life choices. Even I had started to think maybe everyone else was right about me and I'd overestimated my ability to change the course of my life. My self-confidence was low, I attracted a lot of "energy suckers", I had trust issues, and I had a lot of negative voices in my head. *ARGHHHHHHH*, I was screaming inside my calm demeanor. I decided that I just wanted to be alone.

Jason and I struck up a friendship unexpectedly. I found myself drawn to his odd sense of humor that distracted me from my negative thoughts. He was not like other people I'd met. For example, other people would never question me when I told a white lie, but without fail, he would immediately sense I was lying every time and keep asking me questions that would make me fret and promise myself I would never do it again.

Every time I started to tell myself the numerous reasons why certain things couldn't be done, as simple as "it is not worth not looking for an earring" that I dropped at one of the tourist lookouts along the Great Ocean Road. In that instance, Jason said without hesitation, "Failure to search is failure to find!" Then off we went searching. And you know what? Magically, we found it, it's a miracle! I learnt a valuable lesson from him that day—a simple shift in mindset actually does attract "miracles"!

Whenever I was down, beating myself up when things in my skin care business didn't seem to be going anywhere, he would always tell me that he believed in me and that one day I would get there because I worked so hard and I was very passionate about what I was doing, and, "You are helping so many people. Don't forget this, I am your biggest fan, even if I'm the only fan! Together we can make things work." Jason's unwavering support kept me going and often brought me back from self-pity. He was right, being down in the dumps would not change anything, I had better redirect my energy to do something helpful.

Jason and my daughter, Jasmine, have created an artform in making fun and laughing at me whenever I took things too seriously, which I tend to do often. It used to drive me mad, but now I realise it was exactly what I needed to keep myself centered and balanced.

Ubuntu, I am becoming who I was meant to be, doing what I was born to do, fulfilling my destiny because each person I honored here helped lift me up and cheered me on, allowing me to stand on their shoulders along the way to my dreams.

I am very excited and feel confident that I am on the right track, all because of them.

Judy Cheung-Wood

Multi-award-winning entrepreneur Judy Cheung-Wood's vision is to support people to feel confident and well with acne-free skin. She founded SkinB5, a global brand that offers effective, holistic, everyday skin care treatments for healthy skin and acne control.

Knowing what it's like to suffer the pain of teenage and early adulthood acne, Judy's quest to create a highly effective treatment, based on a revolutionary, patented Vitamin B5 formulation, has seen SkinB5 rapidly grow to become a thriving global brand.

SkinB5 is a combination of highly effective, proprietary nutritional supplement formulations and healing skin care products that treat acne as naturally as possible, with zero nasties and without side effects.

SkinB5 is trusted by an increasing number of health professionals as a workable alternative to prescription acne medication.

Unlike other mainstream acne products, SkinB5 addresses underlying nutritional deficiencies and targets the root causes to stop acne before it starts—from within the body first. Thousands of acne sufferers have been successfully treated in this way since 2006.

Customer feedback is strong. Many report that SkinB5 products are "game changers" because they heal both the skin *and* the crushing isolation that acne sufferers often feel.

Judy's maternal grandfather was a chemist and manufacturer of natural skin care products. Inheriting his expertise and passion for traditional, nutritional medicine and his ability to create effective natural skin care products, Judy began her quest to find the solution to her own acne challenges as a young adult. Supported by her grandfather's extensive knowledge and wisdom, she emulated his ways by starting to care for the whole body from the inside first.

Today Judy continues her grandfather's legacy. She's here to make a real difference, by helping acne sufferers heal and flourish. The very heart of the SkinB5 brand is to make effective, natural skin care available, to help users believe in themselves more and confidently present their full face and vision to the world.

SkinB5 is now a successful global company because of Judy's initial courage to hold her vision and move beyond all doubt. When asked to reflect upon her powerful inner drive to help others, Judy credited it to her unusual upbringing and the difficult experiences and relationship she had with her father.

Judy is an author in two anthologies by Oprah's all-time favorite guest and renowned international humanitarian, Dr Tererai Trent: *Sacred Promise* and *Ubuntu*. She also co-authored the *Women Leading the Way* book by Women Changing the World Press.

Born in Hong Kong, Judy spent her early childhood in Honiara, Solomon Islands. An international student in New Zealand and Australia during her teenage years, Judy then lived and worked in California for four and a half years, before returning to Sydney. Judy currently resides in Melbourne, Australia, with her funny, kind and supportive husband Jason, who is also a devoted father to their daughter Jasmine.

Her rich life experience was the foundation for her exceptional open-mindedness, visionary nature, and ability to adapt, see and do new and "different" things and create the global success story that is SkinB5.

Website: skinb5.com
Instagram: instagram.com/skinb5
Facebook: facebook.com/SkinB5
YouTube: youtube.com/user/skinb5video
LinkedIn: linkedin.com/company/skinb5-pty-ltd & linkedin.com/in/ judycheungwood
TikTok: tiktok.com/@skinb5

SUPPORTING A GOOD CAUSE

Proceeds from the sale of this book go towards creating cultural and lasting generational change through investing in girls education.

To invest in girls education, inquire about having Dr. Tererai Trent as a speaker at your next event or learn more about Tererai and her work visit www.tererai.org

9 780645 785845